FOUL DEEDS & SUSPICIOUS DEATHS
AROUND SWANSEA

TRUE CRIME FROM WHARNCLIFFE
Foul Deeds and Suspicious Deaths Series

Barking, Dagenham & Chadwell Heath
Barnet, Finchley and Hendon
Barnsley
Bath
Bedford
Birmingham
Black Country
Blackburn and Hyndburn
Bolton
Bradford
Brighton
Bristol
Cambridge
Carlisle
Chesterfield
Colchester
Cotswolds, The
Coventry
Croydon
Derby
Dublin
Durham
Ealing
Fens, In and Around
Folkstone and Dover
Grimsby
Guernsey
Guildford
Halifax
Hampstead, Holborn and St Pancras
Huddersfield
Hull

Jersey
Leeds
Leicester
Lewisham and Deptford
Liverpool
London's East End
London's West End
Manchester
Mansfield
More Foul Deeds Birmingham
More Foul Deeds Chesterfield
More Foul Deeds Wakefield
Newcastle
Newport
Norfolk
Northampton
Nottingham
Oxfordshire
Pontefract and Castleford
Portsmouth
Rotherham
Scunthorpe
Shrewsbury and Around Shropshire
Southampton
Southend-on-Sea
Staffordshire and The Potteries
Stratford and South Warwickshire
Tees
Uxbridge
Warwickshire
Wigan
York

OTHER TRUE CRIME BOOKS FROM WHARNCLIFFE

A-Z of London Murders, The
A-Z of Yorkshire Murders, The
Black Barnsley
Brighton Crime and Vice 1800-2000
Crafty Crooks and Conmen
Durham Executions
Essex Murders
Executions & Hangings in Newcastle
   and Morpeth
Great Hoaxers, Artful Fakers and
   Cheating Charlatans
Norfolk Mayhem and Murder

Norwich Murders
Plot to Kill Lloyd George
Romford Outrage
Strangeways Hanged
Unsolved Murders in Victorian &
   Edwardian London
Unsolved London Murders
Unsolved Norfolk Murders
Unsolved Yorkshire Murders
Warwickshire's Murderous Women
Yorkshire Hangmen
Yorkshire's Murderous Women

Please contact us via any of the methods below for more information or a catalogue
WHARNCLIFFE BOOKS
47 Church Street, Barnsley, South Yorkshire, S70 2AS
Tel: 01226 734555 • 734222 • Fax: 01226 734438
email: enquiries@pen-and-sword.co.uk
website: www.wharncliffebooks.co.uk

Foul Deeds & Suspicious Deaths Around

SWANSEA

BERNARD LEWIS

First Published in Great Britain in 2009 by
Wharncliffe Local History
an imprint of
Pen and Sword Books Ltd
47 Church Street
Barnsley
South Yorkshire
S70 2AS

Copyright © Bernard Lewis 2009

ISBN: 978-184563-087-4

Typeset in Plantin by Concept, Huddersfield.

Printed and bound in England by CPI UK.

Pen & Sword Books Ltd incorporates the Imprints of
Pen & Sword Aviation, Pen & Sword Maritime,
Pen & Sword Military, Wharncliffe Local History,
Pen & Sword Select, Pen & Sword Military Classics,
Leo Cooper, Remember When, Seaforth Publishing and
Frontline Publishing.

For a complete list of Pen & Sword titles please contact
PEN & SWORD BOOKS LIMITED
47 Church Street
Barnsley
South Yorkshire
S70 2BR
England
E-mail: enquiries@pen-and-sword.co.uk
Website: www.pen-and-sword.co.uk

Contents

Acknowledgments

Much of the research for this book has been by way of the original press coverage in the *Cambrian* newspaper. In that respect I am very grateful to Mrs Marilyn Jones, Local Studies Librarian, Swansea City Council, and her team at the Cambrian Newspaper Index, an absolutely invaluable resource for any historian of nineteenth-century Swansea. Indeed, I would not have accepted the commission to write this book had I not known of the existence of the index.

I am also grateful to Mr Kim Collis and his colleagues at the West Glamorgan Archive Service, Swansea, for their assistance in producing microfilm rolls, documents and photographs and for giving advice with their usual efficiency. Similarly, the staff at the Glamorgan Record Office, Cardiff, and the staff at Swansea's superb new library also provided assistance and guidance.

Friends and colleagues rallied around in various ways to help me. A great friend of long standing, Jim Knight and his wife Pat, kindly gave me the 'Grand Tour' of Pontarddulais and pointed out several memorials with Rebecca Riot connections. Dave Westron allowed me to use images from his photographic postcard collection of Swansea views. Noel Evans, Registrar of Cemeteries and Crematoria at Swansea City Council kindly granted me access to burial records relevant to the yellow fever outbreak at Swansea. Mrs Edith Morgan, Registrar of Births, Deaths and Marriages at Swansea, also provided advice and guidance in my researches.

At the South Wales Police Museum, Bridgend, Ms Terina Shaw of the Visitor Centre kindly gave me permission to use images of numerous items relating to the Victorian police force that are held at the museum. Mr Mark Vivian, at the Mary Evans Picture Library allowed me to use two illustrations from the *Illustrated London News*.

The Penllergare Trust at Swansea – dedicated to restoring the estate grounds of the Llewelyn family – kindly gave me permission to use images that are held by trust member Richard Morris. Richard is a descendant of the Llewelyn family and was very helpful, producing one photograph from as far back as around 1846.

Mr Simon Lee of Cardiff provided me with information on the 1914 case of Sergeant Hopper, a by-product of his ongoing research into the 6th Battalion, the Welsh Regiment, in the Great War. Simon also contributed information to my earlier book on the Swansea Battalion.

Mr Spencer Feeney, editor of the *South Wales Evening Post* granted me permission to use material from its predecessor newspapers, the *South Wales Daily Post* and the *Cambrian*, and similarly the editor of the *Western Mail* granted permission for material from early editions of that newspaper.

Mr Rupert Harding at Pen and Sword Books, who asked me to contribute this volume to Wharncliffe's Foul Deeds series, also deserves a mention. He has been a wise counsel and a source of ready encouragement. The production team at Pen and Sword Books have also produced this book to their usual high standards.

I am grateful to all of the above and extend my warm thanks to them.

Lastly, I must thank my wife, Elizabeth (Lib), for her willing support and cheery forbearance of a house and dining table once again all too often strewn with research papers, and a list of domestic chores that had temporarily been put on hold.

Introduction

Swansea is a city that has undergone a transformation in the last quarter century. Much of the industrial derelication that blighted so much of the city has been swept away to be replaced by an enterprise zone, a marina and modern housing. The city centre is also undergoing major change while the impressive SA1 development is bringing back into use a previously long deserted and derelict docks hinterland.

But while Swansea can look forward to a bright future it cannot escape its darker past. This book seeks to bring back into the spotlight some of the murkier deeds of its long and turbulent history. It covers the often violent actions of the Marcher lords and their enemies, as well as those of the sometimes grasping Tudor gentry. There is a quack doctor charged with manslaughter, a murderous mutiny on a Swansea ship, dangerous foreign sailors at loose in the Strand, and an unprecedented outbreak of deadly tropical disease in the town. Mixed in with these sordid episodes are those of the men who killed their own wives or children, as well as true tales of Rebecca Rioters, common murderers and vicious Victorian street gangs. All have their entrances and exits in Swansea's rich and sometimes brutal history.

Swansea may now be a vibrant and modern city that knows where it is going, but it has not always been so. This book looks back to times when things were not quite so certain and fear frequently roamed the streets. Swansea's iconic poet, Dylan Thomas, famously called it an 'ugly, lovely town' and this book inevitably, given its subject matter, focuses on the ugly side of a lovely town that became a great city.

CHAPTER 1

Swansea Crime: From Medieval Times to the Reign of Queen Victoria

There has been much speculation about the origin of the name 'Swansea' and the possibility that it is linked to the early Scandinavian raiders who terrorised the Welsh coastline and set up a small settlement on the River Tawe. It is, in fact, only from the time of the Norman conquest of South Wales in the early twelfth century that Swansea can be firmly placed on the map. At that time Henry de Beaumont, a trusted aide of Henry I, was handed the lordship of Gower and proceeded to develop his *caput* or headquarters at the mouth of the river Tawe. Thus was the town of Swansea truly born.

A book about foul deeds in a town or locality inevitably comes up against considerable barriers when looking back from Victorian to medieval times. The records are frequently sparse, occasionally in a foreign language and – to the amateur historian at least – are often recorded in an almost indecipherable hand. Additionally, the criminal activities of the mass of the population tended to go unrecorded except where their transgressions were against the property, rights or privileges of the local lord or gentry. It is against this backdrop that some brief examples of crime in Swansea before the age of Queen Victoria are developed on the following pages.

At the centre of the Norman town of Swansea stood the castle. Indeed, it stands there still, having survived the worst efforts of the Luftwaffe to destroy it in the blitz of 1941. The blitz, especially the three days of heavy bombing that occurred in February 1941, devastated the centre of the town and in so doing totally destroyed its largest and most famous department store, Ben Evans and Co. Amazingly, though the castle stood only across the street from this shop, it remained largely unscathed by the falling torrent of high explosives and fire bombs.

In Norman times the castle, which over time evolved from a timber building on a raised knoll to a substantial stone-built

Swansea Castle in 2009. The small dark circle within a lighter square near the top of the tower is a fifteenth-century gun-port, allowing a gun to be aimed down Wind Street.
The author

structure, was the hub of local administration. It was of course primarily a military stronghold and a barracks for the local soldiery. When not travelling around his lordship or even further afield (a time consuming activity in twelfth century Wales) the Lord and his family lived within the castle which had large personal quarters set aside for that purpose. Justice could also be doled out within the castle walls at the manorial courts, and it also acted as the administrative and financial headquarters for the lordship. A prison was included within the walls though this was little more than some uncomfortable rooms. As the focus of the early town, the castle was at the centre of several foul deeds.

Before Henry I handed the lordship of Gower, and with it the castle, to Henry de Beaumont it was in the hands of a Welsh-born lord named Howel ap Goronwy. Howel became a victim of the internecine struggles between the ambitious French-born lords who, post Norman conquest, then held lands in Wales. He was betrayed by Gwgan ap Meurig who, having invited Howel to visit his house, sent word to the French who held the castle of Rhyd-y-Gors. These men surrounded the house and disturbed the sleep of Howel who fled unarmed. He was pursued by Gwgan and his men then caught and taken, half strangled, to the French. They decapitated him.

In 1319 Edward II commissioned an investigation into allegations that the current Lord of Gower, William de Breos, in concert with twenty-three named others, had taken and carried away the goods of John Iweyn, an aide of Hugh Despenser, the Lord of Glamorgan. William de Breos and Despenser were at odds with each other. In 1321 the unfortunate Iweyn was taken from the castle at Neath (where he was joint custodian) to Swansea where he was decapitated, an apparent victim of the lordly power struggles that plagued the Marcher lordships.

King Edward II abdicated in 1326 following a baronial revolt. The desperate former king believed that he would find allies in South Wales and proceeded there in the hope of gathering support to help him resist the barons. He got as far as Neath Abbey before being captured nearby by his enemies on 16 November 1326. He had sent certain court documents on ahead and these had reached the castle at Swansea where they were subsequently confiscated and sent back to his captors. However, it soon became apparent that far more than mere documents had been sent forward and the new king, Edward III, was anxious to discover what had become of

Neath Abbey in 2009. The remains are still impressive, 500 years after the dissolution of the monasteries. The author

the other items that should, by right, have devolved to him. The king therefore appointed an inquisition charged with finding out what had gone missing and how.

The inquisition discovered that the King's goods had been entrusted to the custody of John de Langton who had then taken the items to Swansea. The load had consisted of a great quantity of plate and armour, viz. 200 platters worth £351, one hundred silver saucers, fourteen pitchers, eleven dishes, nine basins, twenty-eight silver cups, eight sleeveless coats of chain mail, seven quilted garments, four beds for the King's wardrobe and several other items. Suffice it to say that of the local gentry Res Dwy was subsequently found to be in possession of royal goods valued at £400 whilst William le Hunte held items to the value of £120. Numerous others had benefitted in various sums. Even the rector of Penmaen had been sent two horses as his share of the ill-gotten loot. His deep rooted religious principles apparently came to play on his conscience, however. He sent one horse back but kept the other. The total value of the hoard was valued by the inquisition at £2,472-9s-11d. Exactly what steps were taken to remedy the situation is not known but it is likely that the un-lawfully taken goods would have had to have been restored to the new King as a minimum requirement.

The castle at Swansea also saw much violence in its working lifetime though it was more in the way of armed conflict than any underhanded foul deeds. For example, in 1116 Gruffudd ap Rees attacked the castle, burning the outer defences though the tower resisted all attempts at capture. Several of Rees's supporters were slain in this unwise endeavour. Twenty years later, in 1136, Gower itself was attacked by unruly neighbouring lords resulting in much loss of life in a pitched battle near Garngoch. Though a great deal of destruction was visited on the surrounding land the castle itself seems to have escaped attack during this incursion.

In 1192 the castle was the object of a ten week siege by forces coming from Dyfed. It was recorded that the town would have been forced into submission due to starvation were it not for the fact that dissension in the ranks of the besiegers led to it being discontinued a little prematurely. Things got even worse after Swansea was burnt by 'Rhys the Fierce' in 1212. By 1215 the castle was held by the king and withstood a ferocious assault led by 'Young Rhys' even though the defenders had been compelled to burn the town to deny it to the enemy. The enemy was undaunted, however, and moved to attack the castle at Oystermouth, which it took by force soon afterwards.

Llewelyn ap Iorwerth of Gwynedd rallied the Welsh princes in 1217 and approached the castle at Swansea which was surrendered

Oystermouth Castle at Swansea in 2009. Situated on a hill overlooking Swansea Bay, the castle is still a significant local landmark. The author

to him without a fight. Llewelyn entrusted the castle to the keeping of Rhys Gryg, who himself had led the fierce attack on it of 1212. Given a free hand Gryg destroyed much of Swansea Castle as well as all the castles of Gower, driving out the English settlers at the same time. It was 1220 before some order was restored and the castle repaired, possibly for the first time in stone rather than wood. This would not be the only time that the defences were strengthened; around 1400 the threat posed by the Owain Glyndwr rebellion led to repairs and improvements to numerous walls, towers and buildings as well as the employment of three men at arms and eighteen archers. This small garrison would have been augmented by the lord's tenants in the event of any attack by Glyndwr.

In the early 1500s it was recorded that part of the castle was in use as a prison and one man was hung there in 1534 and three more in 1536 though the crimes in any of these cases have not come down to us. The castle did not play an active military role in the English Civil War though a store for gunpowder was constructed at that time.

Another source for early Swansea related crimes are the proceedings of the Court of Star Chamber in Tudor times. The establishment of the 'Tudor squire' and his estate had resulted in the creation of a landed gentry that was able to largely monopolise local government appointments amongst their own numbers. These appointments were then often used to oppress the local populace for the benefit of a self-regulating and self-interested clique. The Assizes and the Court of Great Sessions proved impotent in controlling the excesses of these local potentates while the Council in the Marches, another potential restraining influence, was actually packed with the very people that the central government sought to rein in.

The Court of Star Chamber, by contrast, seems to have been remote enough from the disputes it heard to allow it to deliver something more approaching true justice than would have been the case in the local courts. Much of its work seems to have involved difficulties with various boroughs or officials of the Crown. Ecclesiastical issues were also to the fore, due to the legal doubts and uncertainties arising from the dissolution of the monasteries. One method of getting a hearing at the Court of Star Chamber was to allege perjury at an earlier hearing in a lower court. An allegation in that situation went to the Star Chamber for consideration and effectively allowed a second hearing of the case, a ploy that apparently proved frequently attractive to unsuccessful litigants in a lower court. Three Star Chamber cases follow, though regrettably verdicts are not recorded.

During the reign of Queen Elizabeth I, Hopkin Vaughan of Swansea lodged a case at the Court of Star Chamber. Vaughan alleged that he had been assaulted at Llansamlet by Rosser Vaughan, Matthew Jones, Robert Rosser and others. His servants had also been assaulted in Swansea while he himself had been attacked while out of his doublet due to his being involved in a tennis match at the time. Such had been the commotion that the Portreeve and other officers of the town of Swansea had become embroiled in a veritable minor riot. It was alleged that the general rowdiness engendered by this gang of ruffians had even dissuaded people from travelling to Swansea to conduct business.

A further case occurred in the reign of Philip and Mary (1553–1558) and concerned allegations made by Sir Rice Mansell and his son Edward. The complainants seem to have taken possession of prize goods following the loss of a French vessel off the coast at Oxwich, on the Gower peninsula. The prize did not remain in their hands for very long however; they were assaulted by Sir George and William Herbert in company with others, and the recently acquired goods were forcibly removed from their possession. In this skirmish at Oxwich Castle Anne Mansel (Edward's aunt) was struck on the head and killed. The Herbert's were eventually fined and their servant – who had struck the fatal blow – was pardoned.

Another Star Chamber case occurred in 1581 when William Thomas, a saddler, was disturbed while working peacefully in his shop. He was confronted by a group of men, several of whom he recognised. They threatened him with swords and daggers and tried to tempt him out into the street. This he sensibly refused to do so they switched their attentions to his horse which was tethered outside. This they cruelly beat causing Thomas's wife to intervene only for her to be assaulted in turn. As the men left the scene Thomas reported the matter to one of the town constables who then managed to apprehend and arrest two of the perpetrators of the wicked deeds. Before the matter could be brought before the Portreeve of the town however, the constable's good work was undone by his fellow constable, Owen John Sadler, who released the men after declaring that he would answer for them.

It is possible that in this case the errant constable undertook to post a financial bond on behalf of the miscreants, to be forfeited should they misbehave in future. This was sometimes a convenient alternative to a possibly complex and expensive prosecution through the court system. The payment of compensation by the offenders might also resolve an issue before it reached a Grand Jury. At this time, of course, there was no police force or Crown Prosecution Service ready and able to instigate the necessary legal action to rectify a felony or misdemeanour. It fell to the aggrieved party to find a magistrate with enough interest and capability to put the legal wheels in motion, and even then the cost of prosecution fell on the complainant. It must often have been thought to be not worth the bother or expense of pursuing a case, assuming no lasting harm had been done.

A number of cases with a link to Swansea also crop up in the records relating to the Court of Great Sessions. This court had been set up in 1543 as part of the process of unification between England and Wales. There were four circuits in Wales and the one which rotated around Glamorgan, Brecon and Radnor is of most relevance to the history of crime in Swansea at that time. These courts mirrored the activities of the Assize courts in England,

The ruins of Neath Castle. From an illustration by Samuel and Nathaniel Buck of 1741. West Glamorgan Archive Service

meeting typically in April and August, before two judges, for a six day session.

For example, in August 1759 eight men from Swansea were charged with entering Clyne Wood, which was in the ownership of the Duke of Beaufort, without permission. Whether they were foraging for wood or hunting game is not alluded to, but the trespass in itself was enough to bring them before the Great Session judges.

In April 1766 a more serious case arose when a Swansea mason, Richard Willis, was charged with stealing the goods and chattels of George Lillington. Willis had allegedly stolen an earthen jar containing three gallons of wine, a coat, waistcoat and shirt. A sackcloth and apron completed the haul to the value of £4-5s-0d, for which the unfortunate Willis was sentenced to be transported for seven years. Transportation at that time was to the American colonies, that only changing following the American War of Independence in 1776, after which Australia (or Van Dieman's Land) became the usual destination for the guilty.

In April 1775 the case of Mary Thomas (the younger) came before the court. Mary was accused of having secured goods under false pretences though no further detail is given. The sentence of the court was that she be kept in solitary confinement for three months, during which time she could no doubt quietly consider – at some length – the error of her ways.

Thomas Madocks was charged in April 1775 with locking up the door of the public market at Swansea and obstructing His Majesty's subjects from resorting to the market and, once there, from buying and selling beef, mutton and veal. Regrettably no decision is recorded in this case and what was Madock's motive in acting as he did is left unexplained.

Finally, the house of Walter Jones was broken into in March 1793 and a watch and several other items were stolen. The culprits, William Storey, a Swansea carpenter, and Thomas Edwards, a mason, were quickly apprehended and sentenced to be hung. Though it would have been scant consolation to them at the time, both men were acquitted of a separate charge of stealing two silk handkerchiefs, the property of John John. That said, it is not clear whether the death sentences were actually carried out; it is not impossible that transportation might have been substituted on appeal, assuming a pardon was not granted.

The arrival of the nineteenth century brought with it more wide-spread coverage of criminal cases in Swansea than had hitherto been the case, greatly facilitated by the development of local newspapers. Then as now crime sells newspapers and the early coverage of important cases is even more detailed than that offered today. It was also a simpler era, of course, and many trials were understandably brief. Forensics and DNA analysis lay far in the future and, indeed, even things like fingerprinting and crime scene photography had not yet arrived. Many offences were simply never brought to trial due to a lack of evidence. Other cases could be regarded as 'open and shut' since perhaps the offence had been witnessed or there was strong evidence against the accused, e.g. having been found in possession of the stolen goods.

Swansea's first paid constable, John Luce, had been appointed in 1821 though his duties were more to do with the protection of the economic interests of the town's burgesses and corporation than with cracking down on 'normal' criminal activity for the benefit of the entire population. Luce had, amongst other things, the authority to 'Seize all beasts and swine found wondering in the town and to impound them in the common pound . . .'

John Luce, Swansea's first policeman, with the Mumbles lighthouse in the background. South Wales Police Museum

In December 1832 Luce appeared at the Court of King's Bench to answer a charge of trespass brought by a Mr Griffiths. Luce had seized a pig from Griffiths, who was a pig drover, in default of the plaintiffs' failure to pay a penny a pig 'export' fee to the corporation (in this case payment had been due to a Mr Rosser, who rented the right to these dues from the corporation). Griffiths sought to recover the six shillings and eight-pence that he had eventually been compelled to pay to Rosser on the grounds that legally there was no right to make such a charge. Luce was in the dock as the person who had actually detained the pig.

It was noted with amusement (if not by the town's ratepayers who eventually footed the bill for the defence) that this minor case involved a host of witnesses brought up from South Wales, as well as five learned counsel. Counsel for Luce had glibly observed that there were several persons present in court who were prepared to swear that black was white and white was not a colour at all. Hence the defence was duty bound to bring up other witnesses from Wales to show – on oath – the falsity of these statements. Judgement in the sum of six shillings and eight pence was duly found, for the plaintiff, presumably at great expense and inconvenience to all concerned. The pig was not called as a witness.

It was 1836 before a professional police force was established in the town of Swansea and even then the outlying districts were left largely to their own devices. Inspector William Rees was appointed and led a force of only six constables, in reality no better than the number that had been employed on the town 'watch' system which had preceded the creation of the new force. That said, the greater professionalism of the new officers soon helped build up a degree of trust and confidence on the part of the public, despite the on-going niggles over funding and what was seen by some citizens as an attack on their personal freedoms. The duties of the fledgling force were even expanded in its first year; it was required to maintain and man a new fire engine provided by the Norwich Union Insurance Company.

It was in 1843 that the area patrolled was to be finally extended to the whole of the borough, rather than merely the town centre. This was to be facilitated by the appointment of twenty-one additional constables whose role would be to primarily patrol the built up areas around Morriston, where a great many industrial undertakings and worker homes were located. Even then, as an economy measure by a penny-pinching corporation Watch Committee, it was decreed that though the men would be paid they would not be clothed in a uniform. A badge of some description would have to suffice. In fact the process stalled entirely and no extra constables were appointed. By 1844 the force strength had nevertheless risen to one inspector, one first class sergeant, one second class sergeant, five first class constables and six second class constables, making fourteen in all, double the size of the 1836 force, but still hopelessly undermanned for a thriving town like Swansea.

The spendthrift attitude of the corporation Watch Committee contributed to a gradual decline in the quality of men serving with the force and this was reflected in operational efficiency. Matters improved in 1851 when Henry Tate of the Bath police was selected as the new superintendent. Stung by press criticism of the police force the Watch Committee also ceased meddling in police appointments and authorised an increase in manning to nineteen, which included the forces' first detective. The spasmodic patrolling then undertaken on the outer districts of the borough suffered a setback when the forces' only horse died and – old penny-pinching habits apparently dying hard – its replacement was later sold to further reduce expenditure. A horse was then hired on three days a week until the folly of scrimping on this cost was revealed when it was realised that it was, after all, cheaper to simply buy and keep a horse solely for police work.

This then was the embryonic police force that – from around 1840 and onwards – would have to deal with the myriad issues and disputes that arose in a bustling town of around 15,000 souls, and a port that was a magnet for ships and sailors from all parts of the world. It would also have to cope with an influx of people drawn by the opportunities for work in the numerous undertakings around the town that were based on metal processing, coal and transport. Many of these economic migrants were from Ireland, attracted by work prospects but also driven on by the gnawing hunger that resulted from the Irish potato famine. The under-developed infrastructure and governance of the town, a throwback to medieval times, creaked and groaned under these new burdens and squalor, disease, poverty and overcrowding became endemic.

This was a heady mix and some friction between the various social groups was inevitable, frequently leading to potentially explosive incidents. It is against that backdrop that we can now move on to examine some of the cases and events that vexed the local authorities, the police and not least the local populace as the Victorian era in Swansea progressed slowly towards the Edwardian.

CHAPTER 2

The Baron Spolasco and His Miraculous Cures
1838–1858

Oh God, aunt, I am dying – this man's medicine is killing me.

On 24 January 1839 Susannah Thomas left her home in Bridgend in the company of her aunt, Mrs Arnott. They made their way on foot towards the *Wyndham Arms* public house, a short distance that could be covered in about five minutes. While on the way Susannah lent on her aunt for support several times, her face contorted with pain. On arrival at the inn they found their passage blocked by a black man who was apparently a manservant of the person they sought.

The servant explained that if they wished to see the famous Doctor Baron Spolasco of Swansea, they would first have to pay five shillings. Upon payment being made they were ushered into the presence of the Baron who was then handed the money by his servant. A woman told them to be seated while the Baron dealt with his other waiting patients, about a dozen in all, who were already in the room.

When not directly ministering to the afflicted the Baron sat behind a desk on which rested a box of medicines as well as pink, yellow and white papers. They observed the Baron dressing a woman's leg, as well as both legs of John Thomas, the Baron assuring him that, after this treatment and an issue of medicine, he would soon have 'new legs'. After a lengthy wait it was Susannah's turn and she approached the desk. The Baron spoke:

Well my dear you are coming to see the Baron Spolasco. You feel your-self poorly. I see you are, you have a bold eye with a deadly disorder under it.

On being told by Mrs Arnott that Susannah had pain in her side and stomach and had complained frequently over several weeks, the Baron replied simply 'I see it all'. He made no physical examination of the patient whatsoever. Apparently, to someone as skilled and well versed in the healing arts as the Baron, such tiresome routines were entirely unnecessary.

His questioning then turned to financial rather than medical issues and he probed the backgrounds of his two visitors, presumably to gauge what might be a reasonable fee in return for his invaluable services. He was told that Susannah was twenty-two years of age and had been in service until she had become unwell, while her father was a cooper in nearby Cowbridge.

Having presumably satisfied himself on the level of payment that might be affordable to his visitors the Baron stated that his medicine was very dear, and he could not give them anything for under a guinea. Mrs Arnott only had seventeen shillings and sixpence left in her purse but this satisfied the Baron, on a promise of her bringing the balance later. He then provided two pills and one packet of powder, instructing that one pill and half the powder was to be taken that evening and, if required, the remainder on the following morning. The Baron then stated:

> You may bless the hour that the Baron Spolasco came to Bridgend. You will be another person tomorrow. You should pray for me to the Almighty, and you will be better tomorrow.

The following afternoon Susannah was dead, having suffered in great pain for several hours. A coroner's inquest and a magistrates' court would soon charge the Baron Spolasco with manslaughter and remand him in custody to Cardiff Prison.

So just who was this man who had travelled to Bridgend from his home in Swansea to dispense a medicine that now seemed implicated in the death of a young girl? And why would a young, sick girl so willingly entrust her health to his care, with the ready agreement of her aunt and temporary guardian? To put this into context we need to first go back a year to the wreck of the steam ship *Killarney*.

In his published account of the sinking of the *Killarney*, Baron Spolasco stated that he had boarded the ship on 19 January 1838 at Cork, Ireland. He having '. . . been urgently and unexpectedly called to England professionally, to meet with the Agent of a very high personage, with regard to a difficult surgical case . . .' He had also brought on board all his worldly belongings as he intended to set up a medical practice in Bristol, having practised medicine for some time in Cork.

Baron Spolasco in 1840. National Library of Medicine, USA

His property consisted of '... money, and several hundred volumes of the latest and best editions of surgical and medical works – surgical instruments, of the most modern and improved principle, in every department of the art; namely, fifty cases, in value about three hundred pounds – a gig, with harness, and appointments for travelling, complete – several trunks, containing wearing apparel, jewels and jewellery – household furniture ... and a great deal of other valuable property ...'

On board with him were just over twenty other passengers (including his nine-year-old son), a crew of twenty-two, as well as several hundred live pigs and other cargo. Leaving Cork, the ship made its way to Cove and entered the harbour there. The weather was very rough and one attempt to re-enter the open sea to continue the voyage to Britain was abandoned. While the ship was at anchor Spolasco records that he offered fellow passenger Mrs Morrison medical advice on a gratis basis, while he also enter-tained the assembled host on board with some tuneful airs from his musical box.

Finally leaving the harbour at Cove in the evening, the ship soon encountered tumultuous seas and began shipping water at about 2.00 am. A dense mist descended, the engines stopped and – alarmingly – it became apparent to Spolasco that the direction of landfall was no longer known to the crew. Such was the ferocity of the storm that over 100 pigs were washed over the side of the ship. Passengers were now assisting at the pumps but such was the intake of water that these efforts were largely ineffective and the engines were soon flooded again. With the engines eventually restarted after further frantic pumping, land was eventually sighted, raising the faint hopes of those aboard the storm-lashed ship.

Despite the best efforts of the crew the ship was now fast approaching the ragged rocks of the shoreline. Drifting helplessly it finally struck the rocks in Renny Bay, County Cork, and her mid-ships lodged temporarily in a position that allowed some of the sur-vivors (several people having been already washed overboard) to leap onto the relative safety of the rock upon which she foundered. This rock was some way off from the shelter of the shore and those clinging to its limited protection were battered again and again by the heavy seas. The jagged edges of the rock mercilessly cut the hands and legs of those gripping it for safety. At this time Spolasco's son, Robert, was swept away as the Baron bravely struggled to assist his fellow sufferers on their exposed perch. A seaman who attempted to swim to the shore promptly disappeared under the heaving foam and was not seen again.

Two nights were spent trapped on the rock in awful conditions, with neither food nor shelter. Shore-based helpers finally managed to sling a rope between two nearby promontories so that it passed over the rocky crag on which the ship's survivor's still grimly clung. A 'cot' was then attached to the line and pulled out by hawsers to the rock and into the weak grasp of the ragged band of humanity. Spolasco offered to enter the cot first and test the safety of the contrivance. Whether this was bravado or a desperate desire to be first off the rock is unclear (it was of course bravery, later claimed Spolasco, and it was indeed a dangerous and untried procedure). However, he graciously gave way to a female who was then hauled to safety. All still surviving on the rock were eventually brought to shore by this arrangement. Over thirty souls had been lost in this terrible disaster. Spolasco himself was in a poor condition and it was later reported in the Irish press that he had had a leg amputated. Consequently his evidence to an official enquiry into the loss of the *Killarney* was slightly delayed due to his medical condition.

It seems that Spolasco, after recovering and finally reaching Britain, did spend some time practising medicine in Bristol. A newspaper advertisement in 1838 has him at College Green. He put the letters 'MD, MRCS, KOMT and CLD'H' after his name though whether he was entitled to is open to debate. The letters 'CLD'H' might be the award of the 'Knight Order of the Legion of Honour' – a Serbian title of no medical significance. By October 1838 he had announced his arrival in Swansea by way of an advertisement in the local newspaper – the *Cambrian*.

Headed *Qui N'a Sante N'a Rien* ('He that hath health, hath all things') the advertisement went on to say that Spolasco '. . . the most successful Practitioner of Medicine and Surgery in the World!!! . . .' could be consulted at his residence at No. 2 Adelaide Place, Swansea. His stay at Swansea was to be extended so he could deal with '. . . the numerous Patients that daily crowd round [his] consulting rooms . . .' He warned, however, that his return to Bristol could not be long delayed. The advertisement finished with a testimonial from Catherine Smith, of the *Rutland Arms*, Swansea, who described the Baron's cure of her ulcerated leg as 'truly miraculous'.

Though there seemed to be no special coverage of the Baron's mode of entry into Swansea it is known that his later forays into its outlying districts were conducted in some style. In January 1839 it was reported that the Baron had left his residence at Adelaide Place (where the South Wales Evening Post office now stands) in order to bring his medical expertise to the masses:

> . . . *in his elegant travelling chariot and four. His liveries are, indeed, splendid, superb; they are crimson, white, scarlet and gold. The carriage and four horses were the only property the Baron has saved from the wreck of the steamer Killarney . . .*

Similar advertisements appeared regularly in the latter months of 1838 (and beyond). William Jones testified that he had been seen by nine doctors over two years for his ulcerated leg but was cured by the Baron in two weeks. Similarly James Rose's ulcerated leg (apparently a favourite Spolasco ailment) had been seen

EXTRAORDINARY CURE BY THE BARON SPOLASCO,

Worthy the attention of the Public in general, and more especially of Captains of Merchantmen.

CASE of Captain DAYMENT, aged 73, for 50 years Master Mariner, and late Captain of the Brig *Elinor and Grace*, of Plymouth. For four years I suffered the most horrible torments that can be imagined, arising from a dreadfully ulcerated leg, of the most dangerous and malignant description, which was pronounced by every one who beheld it to be *utterly incurable.* I had become entirely hopeless of my ever being restored to a state of health, when, by the earnest entreaties of my brother-in-law, Capt. Lewis Richards, I was induced to come over to Swansea to try the celebrated Baron Spolasco, he having attained such universal celebrity in consequence of the immense number of wonderful cures he has effected. I arrived in the month of June last, and placed myself under the Baron's care, and I rejoice to say that, by his great talent and kind attention me, *my leg is now perfectly cured*, and my bodily health entirely restored. For several years I knew not what a night's rest was, but lived in a state of the most indescribable and agonizing torture, indeed so dreadfully acute were my sufferings that I could not actually bear the weight of a handkerchief on the affected limb, but was compelled to have the handkerchief suspended from the ceiling by means of a line and hook! I feel it as a duty that I owe to the talented Baron and to society in general to return him my most sincere and heartfelt thanks for the astonishing cure he has effected, and also to make this public for the benefit of my suffering fellow-creatures. The cure was completed in about four months.——Dated at Clovelly, Devonshire, Nov. 13th, 1839.

SAMUEL DAYMENT, aged 73.

Witnesses to the truth of the above statement,

LEWIS RICHARDS, Ship-broker, 82, Strand, Swansea.
ROBERT COOK, Devonshire-place, Swansea, and Master of the brig *Betsey*, of Bideford.

Swansea, Nov. 18th.

N. B. It is quite impossible for the immense number of important and astounding cures performed by the Baron Spolasco, to be all inserted in a newspaper advertisement, but he will occasionally publish cures of such importance as the above in the columns of the *Cambrian*, but begs to refer the public to the contents of a small pamphlet just published, containing a vast number of extraordinary cures performed by the Baron. It may be procured of Mr. Prior, 24, Wind-street, and at the Stationers.

A Swansea newspaper testimonial to Baron Spolasco. The Cambrian

admittedly by only two doctors, but without the slightest beneficial effect, his having '... suffered for a very long time ...' before Spolasco again completed the two week cure trick. At this time the Baron was also promoting sales of his narrative account of the wreck of the *Killarney*.

As the advertisements continued to appear the Baron seemed to be in need of some assistance to cope with his apparently heavy caseload. To this end he advertised for two or three articled pupils, each to observe Spolasco's systems for three or five years before setting up in practice on their own account. Only those of a '... good family, education and address ...' need bother to apply. As well as tuition, board and lodging would also be provided. The premium for each pupil was to be 525 guineas (over £551), a considerable sum in 1839. A week later the Baron was to report that several people had offered him in excess of £300 for a pupil-ship but no-one had met his full asking price. He asserted that if any fully paid up 'Pupil of Spolasco', once qualified, failed to recoup the £551 premium in a single year in any town of 20,000 plus souls, then he would make up the shortfall himself. Nothing seems to have come of the idea, however, and Spolasco continued to practise alone.

Spolasco spent some time visiting the other towns and villages around Swansea, always announcing his planned arrival time in the local press. On 2 January 1839 it was stated that he would be at Neath before heading for Merthyr. At the *Star Inn*, Neath Abbey, it was reported that thousands had assembled to see him, while at Hirwaun (as he was merely passing through on route to Merthyr) he was stopped by a gathering '... who one and all, with money in their hands, demanded advice of the great and good Baron Spolasco ...'

It was against this backdrop that Susannah Thomas of Bridgend read in the local newspaper of the planned visit to Bridgend of the famed Baron Spolasco of Swansea, the celebrated physician. At this time Susannah had been ill with abdominal pain for four months and had been seen by a local doctor on several occasions, to little apparent benefit. As was mentioned earlier, after taking the medicine prescribed by Spolasco, Susannah died within about twelve hours, in terrible agony.

Having been remanded in custody at Cardiff Prison on a charge of manslaughter Spolasco stated in a letter from prison to the *Cambrian* of 31 January 1839 that he had not given evidence before

"QUI N'A SANTE, N'A REIN."
"SUNT MILLE MALA, SUNT ETIAM REMEDIA."

MOST IMPORTANT TO ALL CLASSES!

The justly Celebrated and most Extraordinarily-gifted Anatomist, Physiologist, Botanist,
and Chymist of the age, the Great and Good

BARON SPOLASCO,

M.D., M.R.C.S., A.B., A.M., K.O.M.T., and C.L.D'H., &c., &c.

Has arrived in London, where he has been called to attend professionally on a nobleman
of high rank, in order to save amputation in a case where mortification had set in. After
only a few days' attendance on this noble patient, the Baron was satisfied that not only would
the painful operation of amputation be rendered unnecessary, but that the limb would be
restored to its natural strength, and the entire system completely renovated. This will
show the necessity of persons similarly circumstanced making application to the Baron
before undergoing such mutilation, as it has been proved to demonstration, time after
time, that by the system which the Baron adopts, and which is peculiar only to himself,
he can save the limb, be it ever so far gone in mortification.

The BARON SPOLASCO was a perpetual pupil to the late celebrated Baron Dupuytren,
of the Hôtel Dieu, Paris; he has also studied his profession minutely and laboriously at
the Universities of Paris, Berlin, Leyden, London, Edinburgh, Glasgow, and Dublin. He
begs to observe that he is most successful in the practice of midwifery. Expectant suffering mothers, whose child-birth is to them almost worse than death itself, may avoid such
unlimited affliction by timely application to the BARON SPOLASCO.

Innumerable instances of the most interesting and extraordinary cures fully prove him
to be a first-rate and unrivalled scientific Surgical Operator and Bone-setter, and a most
successful practioner in the treatment of sprains and dislocated joints. He even safely
challenges all competition in every department of his extensive profession.

He has been peculiarly successful in the treatment of the following diseases, viz. :—
Consumption, Nervous Affections, Diseases of the Eyes, Gout, Rheumatism, Cholera
Morbus, Billious Diseases, Chlorosis or Green sickness, Agues, Appoplexy, Diabetes,
Diarrhea, Diseases of the heart and stomach, Scrofula, Diseases of the Skin, Asthma,
Sore Breasts, Pleurisies, Sore Throats, Liver Complaints, Measles, Cholic, Croup,
Quinsy, Hysterics, Paralytic Affections, Stone and Gravel, Dysentry, Venereal Diseases,
Jaundice, Small Pox, Flatulency, Lumbago, Fevers, Cancers, White swellings, Cramps,
Seminal Weakness, Scald heads, Convulsions, Boils, Burns and Bruises, Bowel Com-
plaints, St. Vitus's Dance, Colds, Coughs, Costiveness, Worms, Inflammations, Want of
Appetite, Eructations, Leprosy, Abscesses, Nausea, Frightful Dreams, Dropsy, Influenza,
Itch, Epilepsy, Fistula, Gleet, Swellings in the Neck, Strictures, Hectic Affections, Spit-
ting of Blood, Retention of Urine, Fits, Erysipelas, Piles, Heartburn, Contraction of the
Limbs, Ruptures, Insanity. Diseases induced by the injudicious use of mercury, foul
Breath, Lameness occasioned by contraction of the sinews of the knee, though of ever so
long a duration, Syphillis in all its stages, Gonorrhoea, Female Irregularities, Declines,
Debility, Dizziness, Corns, Depraved Vision, Eruptions of the skin, Evil, Head Ache,
Putrid sore throat, Scurvy, Impotency, Stammering, &c. The Tooth Ache, without ex-
tracting, cured by one dose of purifying medicine.

Particulars of many of the Baron's most extraordinary cures may be seen in his
Pamphlet, of 24 pages, which may be obtained *gratuitously*, also, in his Narrative of the
Wreck of the *Killarney* Steamer,† price 2s. 6s., both of which can be had on application,
between the hours of 9 and 2 o'clock every day, at his CONSULTING ROOMS,

131, BLACKFRIARS ROAD,

OPPOSITE THE SURREY THEATRE, LONDON.

A most extraordinary cure was performed by the Baron Spolasco, M.D., &c., in a few
weeks for Mr. RAYMOND, Victoria Pie house, New-cut. So bad was he of Gout, Rheumatism, Rheumatic Gout, and Fever, that he could not bear the weight of the bed clothes
upon him. After the other medical men had signally failed the Baron perfectly cured
him in a few weeks to the astonishment of all acquainted with this great case.

† Perhaps it is not generally known that the Baron and two others are the only survivors
of this dreadful shipwreck, which took place ten years ago, on which occasion the Baron
lost his talented son (nine years old,) and property in gold on board to the amount of
£25,000. His travelling chariot, four splendid horses, and four servants were providentially
saved by being five minutes too late to be taken on board the steamer on that eventful
morning.

A handbill advertising the arrival of Baron Spolasco in London. The Bodleian Library,
University of Oxford (Patend Medicines 21(49))

the coroner or magistrates as he had been refused an adjourn-
ment to the next day so that his solicitor could attend. Therefore
his side of the story remained untold but he now hoped to call
witnesses at his trial to confront '. . . those who swore so recklessly
against me . . .' He remained confident that he would triumph
before an unprejudiced tribunal. He also took the opportunity to
apologize to those patients that he had planned to meet at
Newport, Pontypool, Abergavenny, Nantyglo, Tredegar and
Merthyr, his unwarranted imprisonment making it impossible
for him to attend at those places for the moment.

Spolasco was released on bail from prison on 20 February 1839,
having provided £200 of his own money, and a further £200 in
sureties from others. He noted that this was despite the clerk to the
Bridgend magistrates and Mr Thomas Arnott (a relative of the
deceased) opposing his release.

On 7 March 1839 the Baron Spolasco appeared on a charge of
manslaughter at the Glamorgan Assizes. The story of Susannah's
visit to the Baron was then placed before the court. Mrs Arnott,
giving evidence for the prosecution, stated that on returning home
from the consultation Susannah had taken half of the Baron's
medication, as directed, before retiring for the night at 11.00 pm.
In the morning Mrs Arnott had been disturbed by Susannah crying
out 'Oh God, aunt, I am dying – this man's medicine is killing me'.
The remainder of the medicine was given around midday but no
improvement was discernible. Mrs Arnott stated that she had
never seen Susannah in such pain. Meanwhile, Spolasco was about
to leave the *Wyndham Arms* at Bridgend for the next leg of his
grand tour.

Mrs Arnott found the Baron still at the inn and he suggested that
the medicine would take a little longer to work than usual, as the
girls' insides were weak. He advised plenty of warm gruel, oatmeal
tea and the rubbing of the bowels with a warm flannel though, as
it turned out, this had already been done with no improvement.
Only time would help confirmed the Baron. After a short time
spent back with Susannah, Mrs Arnott again returned to the inn as
things were clearly getting worse. This time the Baron suggested
half a glass of wine and half a glass of brandy, mixed together. This
concoction would at least raise her spirits. Spolasco declined to
visit immediately, saying that he would call on his way out of town.

Though he duly passed the Arnott's house he ignored the wave
of Mrs Arnott as she tried to draw his attention, pausing only to

bow graciously before continuing on his way. By this time Spolasco must have began to worry about the possible consequences of his involvement in what now seemed to be a very serious case, and had decided to make himself scarce. However, the remonstrations of the chasing Mr Arnott finally persuaded Spolasco that a visit might be desirable, after all. On proceeding upstairs Spolasco suggested that Susannah be raised up in the bed and given castor oil and – if that had no effect – a mixture of gruel and turpentine. He said that there was no danger and they were to write to him at Cowbridge (his next stop) and tell him how she was. He would pay the postage for the letter.

By this stage Mrs Arnott recounted that Susannah's feet were cold and beginning to turn purple. Spolasco, however, made no physical examinations or enquiries as to the latest symptoms. He then left the house to continue his journey. Twenty minutes later Susannah was dead. Also giving evidence for the prosecution was John Llewellyn, a surgeon, of Cowbridge. He stated that he had attended the deceased for a period of about a month in the past. He had not, however, seen her in the six weeks leading up to her death. He added that he thought she might have been suffering from dyspepsia and the safest remedy for that was to purge the bowels. Under examination by the defence (which was keen to show that Spolasco had prescribed suitable medicines for the patient) he said that he thought aloes to be a safe purgative. Llewellyn also stated that he had earlier followed a prescription of Dr Nicholls for Susannah, that had included aloes amongst other things. Additionally, had the family given Susannah jalap he would not say that this had hastened her death. Similarly turpentine would not generally be harmful. These comments at least showed that while the Baron's medicines were not 'miraculous' they were at least recognized by mainstream medical practitioners as being helpful in some cases.

The next witness was Mr Verity of Bridgend who described himself as a surgeon though, highlighting the absence of a compulsory system of medical registration at the time, he was not a member of the College of Surgeons. Neither was he a licentiate of the Apothecaries' Hall. What he did claim was the practical experience gained in over thirty years of tending the sick.

Mr Verity had supervised the post-mortem and was assisted by his son and Mr Wood. At the opening of the body it became apparent that Susannah had had serious bowel problems. The peritoneum was inflamed, the small intestines likewise. The stomach itself showed signs of gangrene. A rupture of the stomach was observed, the contents having escaped into the abdominal cavity. Mr Verity deduced that the cause of death was acute inflammation of the stomach leading to gangrene. The stomach rupture meant that the patient was unlikely to live more than perhaps five hours after its occurrence.

The stomach contents were examined and – by taste – Mr Verity believed it to contain aloes as well as jalap mixed with oatmeal. Aloes and jalap were known purgatives. When given by Verity to a dog they had indeed had a purgative effect. In his opinion these substances were not proper remedies for a person suffering from abdominal inflammation. He believed that this medicine, as pre-scribed by Spolasco, had caused extreme abdominal inflammation and shortened Susannah's life.

At this point Mr Llewellyn was recalled. Having listened to the other medical man's evidence he felt that he could not state cate-gorically that the medicines administered by Spolasco might have accelerated the death. They might have but, then again, they might not have. The Judge now intervened, pointing out to the prose-cution that one of its own witnesses (Llewellyn) had expressed a doubt as to whether the medicines had, in fact, accelerated death. It was certain that the defence would seek to call more expert medical testimony that would in all probability cast further doubt on the prosecution case. With prosecuting counsel declining to discontinue the proceedings the Judge suggested that Mr Wood be called, having taking part in the post-mortem examination, and being listed as a witness for the defence.

Wood stated that in his belief the medicines did not cause death though the convulsions and vomiting that Susannah suffered might have caused a rupture of the stomach and an escape of its contents into the abdomen, leading to death from chronic inflam-mation.

At this point the judge stopped the case and addressed the jury to say that they were now being asked to decide which was the correct medical opinion, a task that was beyond their capabilities. They could not do other than to admit to a reasonable doubt at the end of the conflicting medical evidence. On that basis he directed the jury to formally return a verdict of not guilty. The Baron Spolasco was in the clear.

Just over a week after his acquittal Spolasco, realising that despite the favourable verdict his reputation must have been damaged, placed an advertisement in the *Cambrian* in which he stated:

> *... He was perfectly certain as must have been every other person of sound mind, as to the result, but he really does regret that his Lordship deemed it necessary so soon to stop the proceedings by ordering the Jury to find him Not Guilty; not affording him an opportunity of refuting the evidence for the prosecution, having had in court, for three days, near fifty highly respectable witnesses for that purpose; and also to prove the value of his professional services, some of which witnesses have been sufferers in disease for upwards of twenty-five years, under the medical care of their Doctors in town and country; and others having been under the care of the first talent in London, without effect, and who afterwards were speedily and perfectly cured by the Baron Spolasco ...*

He then listed almost about a dozen towns and villages he would be visiting between the 18 and 31 March 1839. Clearly, despite his recent travails, the show would soon be back on the road. In the meantime Verity, Wood and Llewellyn exchanged letters in the *Cambrian*, each attempting to justify his stance at the trial. Mr Wood, MRCS, took apparent pleasure in informing the public that Mr Llewellyn, though calling himself 'Surgeon' in his letter, was actually only a mere apothecary.

So what of Spolasco in future years? The advertisements continued unabated. Indeed, as it became impossible to do justice to the many and wonderful cures performed (or claimed to be performed) by the Baron within the limits of a weekly newspaper, he suggested that the Swansea public might like to obtain a pamphlet he had produced listing them in more detail. This could be obtained (for a small sum) from Mr Prior of Wind Street or from the local stationers. On the first anniversary of his saving from the wreck of the *Killarney* he roasted an ox for the poor of Swansea. He also had minted a brass token bearing his likeness and this was distributed in the areas he visited. His name appeared in the lists as a donor to several local charitable organisations. The Baron seemed to grasp early in his career that 'no publicity is bad publicity'. He was – on the surface at least – very much the successful man about town.

To the BARON SPOLASCO, &c., &c.

DEAR SIR,

PERMIT me through the medium of the widely circulated paper, *the Cambrian*, to thank you from my very heart and soul, for having performed for me a *perfect cure*, in less than a fortnight, without confining me to my bed, or to the house, for one sing e hour; and this, too, after I had tried the *skill* of *three Medical Men*, and other means, without the *slightest effect*. I have now for two years past suffered greatly from a diseased limb, which caused my health to be impaired, and made my heart sick; it was at last my good fortune to meet with Mr. Thomas Gregory, of the *John and Ellinor*, St. Ives, who assured me, " that *I would not get cured without placing myself under the Baron Spolasco*, who had cured him in a month, after six Doctors had failed in ten years trying to do so:" I myself had been under three Doctors, and at the Penzance Dispensary two months, and shared the like fate; and I further believe that I must have suffered to the end of my days had I not had the blessed fortune of coming under your care, to which I would recommend all labouring under any malady, for I am sure you are not only a poor man's friend, but a blessing to the world. I came on purpose to you from St. Ives, and you have, through God's blessing, sent me home well in health, and sound in limb, in a fortnight.

Dear Sir, believe me your obedient Servant,
JAMES DANIEL, Schooner *Industry*, St. Ives.

PUBLIC DINNER
TO THE BARON SPOLASCO.

AT a Meeting of a few of the Friends and grateful Patients of the justly-celebrated BARON SPOLASCO, it was resolved to invite him to a PUBLIC DINNER, to be given to him at the CASTLE INN, SWANSEA, on MONDAY, the 8th day of JUNE next ensuing, for the purpose of congratulating him upon his numerous and well-authenticated CURES, and of thanking him for the wonderful and essential service he has rendered to such vast numbers of the Diseased and Afflicted of the TOWN of SWANSEA and its VICINITY; and for the purpose also of presenting to him a GOLD SNUFF BOX, as a testimonial of their lasting esteem and admiration of his MANY GRATUITOUS CURES performed on the INDIGENT POOR of the above localities.

Tickets may be had at the Bar of the Castle Inn until Friday, the 5th of June, by which period all Tickets must be paid for, and the distribution of them be closed.—Tickets, 5s. each.

Swansea, May 28th, 1840.

A testimonial to the healing powers of the celebrated Baron Spolasco coupled with a notice regarding a public dinner to be held in his honour at Swansea. The Cambrian

In December 1839 Spolasco was again at odds with the authorities. This time the issue was that of him selling medicines on which excise stamp duty should have been levied. It was alleged that the stamps used by Spolasco and glued to the medicine containers he dispensed were forgeries, thus depriving the Customs and Excise of revenue. In opening the case for the prosecution Mr Chilton stated:

> *... I think it justice to the prisoner to explain to you, because I know that his name has made a great noise in this country, and probably I am addressing some who think that he is an extremely useful practitioner; others who probably think that he is impudent quack ...*

After lengthy arguments on the status of the stamps used by the Baron it was stated that '... his Lordship summed up the case to the jury, unfavourably to the prisoner; but the jury, after a long deliberation, brought in a verdict of "Not Guilty".' He was off the hook again.

There was further trouble for the Baron in November 1843 when – with chilling echoes of the Susannah Thomas case – he was again involved in a coroner's inquest. On this occasion the deceased was the Reverend Edward Matthews Davies of Park Place, Gower. The evidence revealed that the Reverend Davies had met Spolasco at a Gower sale and had been persuaded to call on him at his Swansea consulting rooms. A servant of the vicar was a witness and stated that she saw her master pay the Baron five shillings as an 'entrance fee'. A little later the Baron explained that the entrance fee was just that – it simply got you in. His 'consultation fee' was a guinea. This sum was also paid over. After the actual consultation then it turned out that Spolasco's fee for doing something practical to help cure the problem – beyond the simple consultation itself – would be a further twenty guineas. The Reverend gentleman could actually only come up with £12, which the Baron gratefully accepted.

On the way home the Reverend Davies complained of being unwell, though he had not, as yet, even tried the powder and pill prescribed by Spolasco. Just over a day later, with the patient obviously in a serious condition, Spolasco's medicines were duly administered. Within a few hours Davies began retching and continuing to experience severe abdominal pain. He expired on 26 October 1843, just over a day after his consultation with the Baron.

As it turned out the case was clear cut. A post-mortem examination revealed a large tumour and the medical men agreed that Spolasco's ministerings had done nothing to worsen a long standing and finally fatal condition. It was therefore found that the Reverend gentleman had died '. . . by the visitation of God, in a natural way of the diseases and distempers aforesaid . . .' It was also noted that '. . . however culpable it might be to extort money from the pockets of a person labouring under a deadly disease, by pretending to be able to cure him, yet a Coroner's jury could not deal with the case, unless it was proved that death had been caused by the medicine prescribed . . .'

Perhaps at this stage Spolasco realised that the detail contained in the inquest report could only damage further his standing in the Swansea locality. In any event at around 1845 he seems to disappear from the local landscape. He reappeared briefly in Gloucester in 1848 at a court case where it was alleged that he had failed to maintain a child he had fathered. He gave his full name as 'Baron John William Adolphus Gustavus Frederick Spolasco' and disputed that he was the person named in the warrant, one 'John Williams' (also known as Baron Spolasco). The court, however, knew Baron Spolasco when they saw him and proceeded to hear the case which was promptly proved. As the *Gloucester Journal* explained '. . . after some discussion, and not a little theatrical display, the Baron finally consented to pay the arrears to the young woman, amounting (for thirteen weeks) to £1-18s-10d'. This amount having been paid into court the police superintendent returned to Spolasco the gold watch he had held as a guarantee of his appearance at the court. Also in 1850 he advertised his being available for consultation at '. . . 131 Blackfriars Road, opposite the Surrey Theatre . . .' in London.

So by 1850 Spolasco was certainly in London. In fact, the birth of a daughter (Emma Spolasco) had been registered in 1850 to 'William Spolasco' in Stepney, London, the birth having actually occurred in October 1849. The Spolasco surname seems to be exceedingly rare and it is hard to believe that 'William' is anyone other than the Baron himself and that he arrived in London in 1849.

Later in 1850 he appears as 'Baron Spolasco, MD,' in Ward 7, District 1 of New York, having apparently crossed the Atlantic. This American census states that he was born in England, was aged thirty-nine (meaning a year of birth of around 1811 which

Plaque to Baron Spolasco. The panels quote words from a poem of 1840 written about the Baron – and possibly by the Baron! The author

seems a little late for him) and has him listed as an MD. There was a nine year old girl living with him, named as Julia M Nevert. This is possibly the child that Spolasco had been obliged to pay maintenance for back in Gloucester though this is by no means certain. There is no mention of Emma Spolasco. In 1854 another child was born in New York and was named William Spolasco. It is unclear whether this was a child born to, or adopted by, the Baron but that there is a link is undoubted; the Spolasco surname appears only where the Baron is present in a town or country. William went on to become a New York policeman and was cleared of a charge of extortion in 1900.

While in New York the Baron Spolasco came to the attention of American literary legend Walt Whitman (1819–1892). At one time Spolasco stayed at the *St Nicholas Hotel,* near Broadway and advertised himself as an 'MD' in the local trade directories and it is in that locality that Whitman observed him. Whitman unflatteringly wrote of him:

> *Somebody in an open barouche, driving daintily. He looks like a doll; is it alive? We'll cross the street and so get close to him. Did you see? Fantastic hat, turned clear over in the rim above the ears; blue coat and shiny brass buttons; patent leathers; shirt frill; gold specs; bright red cheeks, and singularly definite jetty black eyebrows, moustache and imperial. You could see that from the sidewalk; but you saw, when you stood at his wheel, not only the twinkling diamond ring and breastpin, but the heavy, slabby red paint; and even the substratum of grizzly gray under that jetty dye; and upon our word there's a hair of the same straggling out under the jaunty oiled wig! How straight he sits, and how he simpers, and how he fingers the reins with a delicate white little finger stuck out, as if a mere touch were all – as if his whole hand might govern a team of elephants! The Baron Spolasco, with no end of medical diplomas from all sorts of universities across the ocean, who cures everything immediately; you may consult him confidentially, or by letter if you choose. It would be worth money to see that old gentleman – they say he is nearly eighty – undress himself! Clothes, wig, calves, stays, moustache, teeth, complexion – what a bald, bare, wizened, shriveled old granny he would be!*

The *New York Herald* ran the usual advertisements describing the Baron as being '... from London, of European fame ...' He was, of course, '... performing more important and astounding cures – of every disease ...', outlining one case where Spolasco triumphed where twenty-nine other doctors had failed.

In June 1858 the Baron Spolasco died in New York. The *Gentleman Magazine* was quoted in the *Cheltenham Examiner* as follows:

*The last of the (Quack) Barons. Baron Spolasco, a quack doctor, well
known in Gloucestershire and South Wales, recently died in NY. The
Baron, whether truly or not we cannot say, used to parade in his bills,
in the way of recommendation, that he had escaped from the wreck of
the Killarney steamer, and by a grand appearance and great imped-
ence he contrived to get a great many dupes, and to make a great deal
of money. Frequently he made his appearance in a carriage drawn by
four horses, with postillions, hired to make a sensation; he was the pink
of fashion in dress, but occasionally wore a mountebank costume. His
humbug, however, lasted only for a season, although it was a pretty
long one, and he then took his departure for the United States, and here
he seems to have fallen into poverty before he 'shuffled off this mortal
coil'. 'His first official appearance here was majestic', says the NY
Daily Tribune. 'An office under the St Bobolink Hotel; clean kid
gloves; out driving every day; the coronets on the harness replated; the
brims of the hat curling like the top of a Corinthian pillar. This lasted a
short time, when some difficulty about rent occurred with his landlord
(an unreasonable person), and the Baron moved a little lower down in
the scale of appearances. From this time he kept continually changing
his residence, which grew smaller and smaller every time – and then he
disappeared altogether . . .*

The *Cambrian* repeated an article from the *New York Daily Tribune*,
which was a little tongue in cheek, and referred to the Baron
Spolasco as 'Baron Sparardrap' (Sparardrap is a type of adhesive,
medical plaster). The report gives a further interesting insight into
how Spolasco presented himself to the world. Described by the
Cambrian as the 'notorious Spolasco' it went as follows:

*Who is this pacing slowly down by the Bunkum House, swinging his
cane, and attired in the combined costumes of several centuries? That,
my friend, is the well-known Doctor Baron Sparardrap. You will
observe that he is got up to attract attention. That hat with its curled up
rim is made on a special block for himself. That wig and moustache
and those eyebrows are of a preternatural black, which, contrasting
with the face painted with Otard's best red, make him look somewhat
like those ferocious individuals that pop out of little boxes, imperious
with carmine and horsehair . . .*

*. . . [when in Cork] Baron Sparardrap then suddenly made his
appearance among the astonished Corkonians in a Phaeton drawn by
four black horses, with coronetted harness – a portion of which he still
retains – and a black musician playing Kate Kearney on a key-bugle*

in the back seat. He announced that from purely philanthropic motives he had visited that benighted region for the purpose of curing all the disease which the Corkonians were capable of getting up.

... Some years afterwards, Sparardrap appeared in London, but with a reduced equipage. He used to drive a funny cabriolet in the Park with one horse, and still the coronetted harness ... I believe he had to disappear from that city in consequence of a charge of malpractice; but he left to reappear, to my great astonishment, in New York. Here he has driven an equivocal trade for some years ...

Over 150 years after his death he remains unforgotten in his adopted town of Swansea; alongside the statues raised in the city to the numerous scions of Swansea society nestles a series of wall plaques dedicated to the memory of 'Baron' Spolasco. Not one of the great and the good, but one that can simply never be forgotten, despite his dishonest practices. The plaques adorn an arch in Swansea's maritime quarter, created in the 1980s, and present a relief portrait of the Baron as well as numerous panels that record his activities in Swansea and elsewhere, and also recount his actions in the wreck of the *Killarney*.

Was he a Baron? Definitely not. There is no mention of the title in Burke's Peerage. Was Spolasco his real name? Probably not. The name only appears in the 1841 British census when it names the Baron Spolasco, and again in the New York census of 1850, after he had apparently emigrated to the United States. There is some evidence to his having been born as the rather less grand sounding 'John Smith' in Manchester, around 1795 and the magistrates at Gloucester had named him as plain 'John Williams'. It is also said that he fled his practice in Southern Ireland for Britain after receiving thrashings from two of his less than satisfied (and certainly not cured) clients.

Was he a charlatan? Yes. Many of his advertisements were probably comprised of false testimonials, composed by 'the Baron' himself. No doubt a number of his patients did in fact recover naturally after (or despite) the treatment they had received from the Baron, only adding to the legend. But the manslaughter trial evidence revealed that he was using 'normal' rather than 'miraculous' medicines and his medical qualifications were bogus. Desperate people still flocked to his door, however.

One source states that the Baron had been buried in the Green-Lawn cemetery in New York. A check of the online indexes, however, failed to find him. In death as in life, the Baron still remains an elusive enigma. It is tempting to wonder if he conducted himself in his final resting place in the cemetery as he had done throughout his life of grand quackery. Stayed a few years and then moved on?

The writer of the article in the *New York Daily Tribune* referred to earlier, finished his largely sceptical and critical article by referring to the wreck of the *Killarney* and by seeing the better side of the great charlatan. Perhaps it would be charitable to do the same. The journalist said of Spolasco:

> *. . . but I never see his queer hat and outre figure, that the vision of that sea-beaten rock does not rise up before me, with its crowd of clinging, shrieking denizens, and the poor quack doctor, with his brave, manly heart, shaming them all in that hour of extremity and peril . . .*

Let him rest in peace. Wherever he is . . .

CHAPTER 3

The Fighting Welsh and the Killing of John Bowling 1842

... the blackguard is dead enough now ...

On 16 August 1842 the *Rising Sun* public house at Swansea was doing its usual brisk trade. Among its customers were local men Rees Griffiths, William Davies, David Rees and William Thomas. All four of them were already known to the legal system. Rees Griffiths – despite being described as a 'boy' – had been charged at the recent assizes with an offence of cutting and stabbing but had been acquitted on the direction of the judge. That was not to say that Griffiths had no case to answer, but rather that the indictment had been poorly drafted and was in fact legally flawed, leading to the discharge of the accused.

William Davies was a native of Penclawdd, near Swansea, a village famed, even to the current day, for its cockle bed harvests. Perhaps unsurprisingly, Davies had attracted the nickname of 'Will Cockles'. He was twenty-nine years old and stood at five feet and seven inches tall. Married at fifteen years of age, he was alleged to have conducted a dissolute and debauched life, and had been previously imprisoned at Swansea for assaulting his wife. His routine treatment of the unfortunate Mrs Davies was described by observers as 'barbarous'.

David Rees answered to the name of 'Dashy' and was twenty years of age and five feet seven and a half inches in height. Born at Morriston, Swansea, he was known to be a former member of a juvenile gang that in 1835 had broken into a local store house, resulting in the subsequent arrest and imprisonment of all participating gang members. Rees had been one of those imprisoned, at the tender age of just thirteen years.

Last of the drinking companions was Swansea-born William Thomas, also known as 'Crib', apparently on account of his skill and daring as a boxer (Tom Cribb was a famous bare-knuckle fighter of the recent past). Thomas was twenty-seven years old and stood at five feet three and a half inches tall. Employed at the local copper works at one time, over the previous ten years he had been imprisoned several times following charges of assault.

Another of the group's cronies, John Lewis, was not present at the *Rising Sun* on what would prove to be a fateful and violent night. Lewis was a labourer of eighteen years of age and was known as 'Shony Tycoch', the Tycoch being the name of his grandfather's farm. Lewis had lived in Swansea all his life and had spent some time in the Greenhill area, an area with a high concentration of Irish immigrants. His capacity for morality and virtue was described as, at best, 'threadbare'.

The final member of this evidently unhealthy alliance was John Evans, who was also known as 'Johnny Backward'. He was eighteen years old and stood at a diminutive four foot eleven inches in height. Perhaps his compact size and low centre of gravity contributed to his main claim to fame – he was notorious as being the best 'jigger' or dancer in the neighbourhood of Swansea's Jockey Street, and this prowess apparently made him a magnet for the local ladies. When not jigging with the ladies he was employed as a shoemaker.

The party left the *Rising Sun* in two groups. Rees Griffiths and William Davies left together and retired to Davies's home in a court at Bethesda Street. A little later they were joined by John Evans, David Rees and William Thomas. The drinking session was not yet over, however; Griffiths had taken three pints of beer to Davies's home.

Bethesda Street was a run-down area of Swansea, with a predominantly Irish population, many of them drawn to Swansea by the work opportunities and the problems of their home country. The drinking continued at Davies's home and the mood apparently darkened, for reasons unknown.

Timothy Leary, an Irishman, also lived at the court and his wife seems to have spent a short time at Davies' house, leading her husband to question her virtue, not apparently for the first time. Voices were raised as this domestic tiff developed. Leary was then approached outside his home by William Thomas, who asked for some snuff. Before Leary could properly respond he was set on by John Lewis and David Rees, who struck him without provocation on the face and left arm. He found no aid or shelter at William

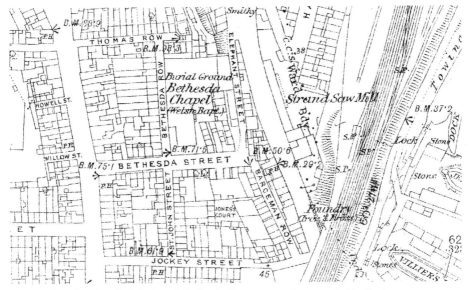

Map showing the location of Bethesda Street. West Glamorgan Archive Service

Davies' house into which he had stumbled as David Rees entered after him and struck him again. Leary then ducked back into his own house and emerged holding a hatchet. This was promptly wrested from his grasp by several gang members and he hastily retired once more to the safety of his home, securing the door behind himself for security.

Living in the same court at Bethesda Street as William Davies and Timothy Leary was another Irishman named John Bowling, aged twenty-four, together with his wife Catherine, and their two young children. The family had lived in Swansea for several years, though they had resided in the court for only two weeks. All the other court residents were also Irish, with the exception of William Davies. Mr Bowling had no current employment and this was reflected in the paucity of the home furnishings; there were none. A plank propped up on stones provided the only comfort, such as it was. Consequently, the couple and their children were compelled to sleep on straw spread over the floor.

On the night in question John Bowling had paid a social visit to the home of his Irish neighbours, Thomas and Honoria O'Connor. Thomas O'Connor had been an occasional workmate of Bowling until unemployment intervened. They were joined a little later by Bowling's wife, Catherine. After a short period Bowling – who was quite sober observed Mrs O'Connor later – left the house and went through a passage in the court, possibly being intrigued by what was probably the sound of the Leary's quarrelling. While the other two ladies chatted on the doorstep they were approached by gang member William Thomas who said to Mrs Bowling 'You are the very woman I want'. Advised by Mrs O'Connor to have nothing to do with the uncouth ruffian, Mrs Bowling returned quickly to her own home.

The door of the Bowling home was of the 'stable door' type, in that the bottom half could be secured while the top half remained open. Mrs Bowling had secured the lower half of the door when she was again approached by William Thomas, who grabbed hold of her and made his intentions clear, exclaiming 'You Irish whore. I wish I was in bed with you for half an hour'. Despite being asked to depart immediately it became apparent that Thomas was intent on entering the house of Mrs Bowling. Encountering spirited resistance to his unwelcome advances, Thomas struck Mrs Bowling who in turn retaliated by hitting him on the head with a piece of brick. At this point John Bowling returned to his home.

'What noise about my house? What's the matter, boys?' asked John Bowling, obviously concerned and confused at the commotion (it was now approaching 1.00 am in the morning). David Rees, standing nearby, responded 'You shall soon know, you Irish bugger'. As the rest of the gang appeared and crowded around Bowling, David Rees produced a hatchet and struck him on the head with the back part of it. With Bowling prostrate, his wife tried to protect him from his assailants but was unable to prevent them roughly picking him up and bundling him into the house. There they set about him with kicks and punches while William Thomas wielded a knife with apparently murderous intent, and William Davies suggested they '. . . kill the Irish bugger . . .' Mrs Bowling implored John Lewis – who stood nearby holding a candle – to save her husband but received no assistance from that quarter. In attempting to protect her husband Mrs Bowling received several blows herself including a knife wound in her lip from William Thomas.

John Lewis extinguished his candle by cruelly inserting it into John Bowling's nostrils – an action that elicited no reaction whatsoever from the stricken man – Lewis stating as he did so '. . . the blackguard is dead enough now . . .' Another neighbour, Ellen Halloran, went to Bowling's house in time to see Thomas using the knife while Rees made further use of the hatchet. At the same time Davies, Evans and Griffiths contributed further kicks and punches. As the men left the house Rees Griffiths encountered and grabbed hold of Thomas O'Connor by his shirt, telling him 'You lousy bugger, we will serve you just like the other man ...' He then kicked O'Connor and was joined by the others who added kicks and punches of their own until the pleas of O'Connor's wife seemed to finally have some calming effect.

At this point Doctor Bird, Mr Rees and Police Constable William Webb arrived and William Thomas, John Evans and William Davies – all found in a nearby house (this was O'Connor's house) – were immediately taken into custody. William Thomas stated to Police Constable Webb 'I know I am in a mess'. By this time the commotion had resulted in the gathering of a crowd of onlookers and the three men were escorted through the throng to the police station. William Thomas commented that 'It was not I that killed him – it was Dashy' (David Rees). Inspector William Rees apprehended John Lewis, who had attempted to hide in the docks area. He was found on the graving bank, cowering under the side of a vessel.

George Gwynne Bird. A well known Swansea doctor, he was also surgeon to the Swansea Prison for a period. The Medical Circular, 1853

Inspector Rees had Lewis placed in the same cell as John Evans. Lewis said to Evans 'You struck John Bowling several times on the back part of the head, with the hatchet'. Evans made no response. It would be a further three months (November 1842) before Rees Griffiths was brought into custody, having been eventually captured near the new pottery.

The sorry tale of the night's events was to be laid before the coroner's inquest which soon followed. The detained men were marched – in irons – from the police station to the town hall through a large crowd of interested bystanders. To the credit of the crowd – given the opportunity presented to it for verbal or physical abuse of the five men – no disturbance took place. It was apparent that the prisoners displayed great coolness and self possession throughout the journey, seemingly quite unconcerned at the serious situation they found themselves in. Indeed, they exhibited what was seen as a disgusting effrontery. By contrast, the friends and relatives who had visited them seemed greatly affected by their predicament. The crowd at the town hall grew to several thousands, such was the interest in the case.

At the inquest the grim facts were recounted to the twelve-man jury. Doctor George Gwynne Bird reported on the findings of his post-mortem examination of the body. He found that Bowling's body had been of a healthy appearance, if due allowance was made for the effects of his beating. On the left temple was a cut that ran for one and a half inches, evidently occasioned by a sharp instrument. This cut went to the bone but had not penetrated it completely. Under the left ear he observed the result of what he felt must have been a tremendous blow, while the chest showed two or three cuts, probably caused by a penknife. An examination of the brain of the deceased revealed a severe injury that the doctor thought was the result of a blow from a blunt instrument or a violent kick. The brain injury was undoubtedly the cause of death.

In due course the prisoners were asked if they wished to add anything to the proceedings, being warned at the same time that anything that they did say would be taken down in evidence. David Rees claimed that he had not touched Bowling and William Thomas claimed likewise. William Davies stated that Rees Griffiths (who at this time was not in custody) had said that he would attend the inquest and confirm that Davies himself was innocent of any offence. Griffiths, however, did not show up on the day (and would not be captured until November). John Evans advanced the idea that he had been a mere bystander while David Rees had attacked both Leary and John Bowling, and William Thomas had struck Mrs Bowling. He also asserted that he had seen Bowling lying on the bench and 'snoring' rather than being 'dead'. John Lewis stated that he had only taken a candle to Bowling's home in order to see more clearly. He recalled seeing John Evans using the hatchet until relieved of it by Rees Griffiths. He did not know what Griffiths did with it.

After these interesting depositions the coroner went over the evidence in some detail before asking the jury to retire and consider their verdict. After an hour's earnest deliberation the jury members returned and recorded that they found the prisoners guilty of wilful murder. That being the case, the prisoners were committed to the House of Correction to await their trial at the Spring Assizes.

The trial took place on Monday, 27 February 1843. Thomas, Evans and Griffiths were defended by Mr Wilson while Mr Nicholl Carne defended David Rees. The accused, William Davies, relied on the advocacy of Mr Richards while, finally, Mr W H Smith defended John Lewis. Mr Sergeant Jones appeared for the prosecution. The Sergeant then recounted the sorry tale of the night of 16 August 1842 and the savage actions which had led to the death of John Bowling. Those present in the dock now stood accused of wilful murder. What slight variations occurred between the evidence that witnesses had given at the inquest and what they might say today could be simply explained said Jones. At the inquest (held a day after the killing) the witnesses were still in an understandably agitated state of mind and due allowance must be made for unimportant variations of detail that might be presented to the jury today.

Jones suggested that the crime had occurred because of ill feeling between the defendants (who were all Welsh) and a growing Irish community in Swansea, of which Bowling was a member. He was certain that the jury would conclude – after the evidence had been heard – that the accused had all been a party to the fateful act. Who had struck the fatal blow or, indeed, which blow had actually caused death was unimportant; the blow of one could be deemed to be the blow of all in cases such as this. On that basis it would be the duty of the jury to convict all as, in point of law, all would be equally guilty.

The defence lawyers homed in on apparent inconsistencies in the evidence of witnesses. If their trial evidence differed from that given at the earlier inquest how could the jury know what was in fact the truth? For example, Mrs O'Connor was pressed on why her trial evidence was more fulsome than that given at the inquest? She replied that it was simply because she was not questioned as much at the inquest. She also stated that her memory was much better now than in the immediate aftermath of the killing. Though she did not know the names of the men at the time of the incident she was certain of their features; they were the men who now stood in the dock.

Mrs Halloran was questioned on her identification of the prisoners while they were held at the House of Correction. She was sure on this point and was backed up by William Cox, deputy governor at the House of Correction, who confirmed that Halloran had correctly identified all concerned. Timothy Leary denied that he had been the worse for drink and had threatened the accused with the hatchet until it was taken off him. His use of the hatchet had been purely defensive in nature; had things escalated he intended to defend himself and his wife with it.

With the prosecution case eventually concluded and cross-examination complete, Mr Wilson rose to address the jury on behalf of Thomas, Evans and Griffiths. He contended that as Doctor Bird had stated in his evidence that the fatal blow had in all probability come from a hatchet or similar implement, then his clients were innocent of murder since, though they had been involved in the melee, they had not used the hatchet themselves. This meant that it was David Rees who was, in fact, the guilty party. It was not, after all, the fault of Wilson's clients that they had committed a minor offence of assault in the company of a man – Rees – who had committed a far more serious offence that had resulted in a fatality.

Mr Carne, on behalf of Rees, was aghast at the suggestion that his client bore sole responsibility for the death. At the end of a very able speech, that reflected potential guilt back on all the accused, he implored the jury to dwell on the awful responsibility that would accrue to them were they to find the group guilty. Six young men would face the death penalty and this was a weight that the jurors would bear for the rest of their lives. He reminded them that all human tribunals were prone to error and stressed that the best laws were those that tempered judgement with mercy. Mr Richards for Davies and Mr Smith for Lewis then made eloquent speeches in turn. All counsel called witnesses who gave evidence of the previous good characters of the accused.

The judge then summed up the case in some detail, taking care to point out to the jury that several legal precedents quoted by the defence advocates were quite inappropriate to the circumstances of the current case; it would be quite proper for all to be found guilty of murder, irrespective of who had struck the fatal blow. The jury then retired and – to the apparent surprise (and not a little dismay) of the judge – returned after a short period of deliberation to render a verdict of 'manslaughter' against each of the accused.

With none of the guilty opting to make any statement to the court before sentence was passed the judge observed:

> *You have been found guilty of manslaughter, and there is not the least doubt but that you are guilty of having killed an inoffensive young man. The jury have put the best construction upon, and taken a most lenient view of, your case. I do not exactly find fault with their verdict – it is their verdict, and not mine. Though your case is somewhat better than that of a murder committed in consequence of long and premeditated rancour, yet I cannot confess how it can be termed manslaughter. I feel it to be my duty to tell you, that in point of law, it is not manslaughter. Here is a harmless young man returning to his house, and upon hearing a quarrel between some person and his wife – who had sufficient cause for defending herself – naturally asks 'What is the matter,' and is answered by being brutally struck on the head with a hatchet, and the others, instead of expressing any detestation of the act, any horror at the crime, all disgracefully rush upon him, more like savage beasts than inhabitants of a Christian country. The sentence of the Court is that you be transported beyond the seas for the remaining term of your natural life.*

The verdict was greeted with surprise by all those present in the court. It is impossible to understand the reasoning of the jury which, of course, was conducted in private and remained so after the verdict was delivered. Was there a racist element to the decision? The arrival in Swansea of many Irish people who were fleeing the harsh economic plight of their home country had added to the social demands already present in Swansea and its local population. Was this 'competition' for already scarce resources a factor in the case?

Were the jury members perhaps swayed by the character witnesses who spoke well on behalf of the accused, despite them being previously known to the law? Did the jury see an element of self-defence in a situation where an Irishman emerged into the street armed with an axe, even if he was quickly disarmed and the hatchet subsequently employed on one of his fellow countrymen? All questions which must today remain unanswered, of course.

If it seems that the sympathy of the jury had veered a little too far in the direction of the accused then it must also be noted that there was considerable sympathy abroad in the town for Mrs Bowling, widow of the deceased, and her two young children. This is evidenced by the fact that less than two weeks after the verdicts were delivered a public subscription set up for the benefit of the family had raised over £30, a not inconsiderable sum in 1843. The fund was intended to assist Mrs Bowling in moving to temporary accommodation prior to her return to the comfort and succour of her native Ireland. Contributions were made by several prominent Swansea citizens. Names listed included J H Vivian, George Grant Francis, the Reverend Doctor Hewson, John Morris, Bart., and even Mr Cox of the House of Correction. No doubt these personages were moved by compassion; but was it also compassion tinged with not a little guilt at a seemingly perverse verdict?

CHAPTER 4

The Rebecca Rioters at Pontarddulais

1843

Great, and I hope salutary, examples must be made.

On the night of 6 September 1843 two of Swansea's foremost citizens, John Dillwyn Llewelyn and Lewis Llewelyn Dillwyn, both local magistrates, found themselves crouching down in a field, under the cover of a hedge, outside the village of Pontarddulais, near Swansea. Both men were armed. They were not, however, pursuing traditional country pastimes by hunting game or rabbits; their prey on this occasion was of the human kind. They were accompanied by a small number of well armed police constables who were under the direction of Captain Charles Frederick Napier, the Chief Constable of Glamorgan. They were located two or three fields away from the Pontarddulais toll-gate.

Information had been received by Captain Napier that led the waiting party to believe that the tollgate on the road at Pontarddulais was about to be attacked by a band of men intent on, amongst other things, opening up the gated road so as to allow free passage and the avoidance of a toll charge by travelers. This was at the height of a series of disturbances in South West Wales that had started in 1839. The men who were engaged in breaking the gates had become known as the 'Rebecca Rioters'. What was not known by Napier was that while he waited to spring a trap on the Glamorgan side of the River Loughor, the Llanelli magistrate William Chambers (Junior) was making similar plans on the Carmarthen side of the river, utilizing a small force of Dragoons and infantry. Chambers' concern was the safety of the toll-gate at Hendy, a hamlet that lay close to Pontarddulais. Both men were blissfully unaware of the others' location and intentions.

John Dillwyn Llewelyn in a very early Daguerrotype image of around 1846. Llewelyn was a pioneer in the art of photography as well as a noted landowner and industrialist. The Penllergare Trust

The 1830s and 1840s were a time of economic depression in Britain. In the largely pre-industrial landscape of South West Wales of that time poverty was endemic, especially in the rural areas. Indeed, such was the seriousness of the situation that the apparatus of the Poor Law, established as long ago as the reign of Queen Elizabeth I, had had to be seriously overhauled by Edwin Chadwick and his associates, resulting in the Poor Law Amendment Act of 1834, which established the much hated workhouse system.

Matters were exacerbated around the 1840s by the failure of successive harvests and a collapse in food prices at the local markets. Staple products were beyond the reach of the impoverished population and prices had to fall to find a buyer who could afford to purchase items, even at rock bottom prices. Added to the existing trials and travails of the struggling poor were even further burdens. The Poor Rates had increased to help fund the newly required and much despised union workhouses, a direct result of Chadwick's Poor Law Act. At the same time parochial tithes had also risen, increasing the pressure on already limited family budgets. If these matters were not crushing enough, the issue of turnpike toll roads and their associated charges also came to particular prominence during this period.

At a time when the roads and streets of many towns were often ill-paved or even not paved at all, the situation in the countryside was far worse. With an increasing volume of wheeled traffic the necessity of continual repair and improvement of the burgeoning road network became a pressing priority. However, the Government chose to leave such issues to the care of the hopelessly underfunded local parishes. The result was that many rural roads were in an awful condition and travel became increasingly difficult, especially in the countryside, and at times of inclement weather.

Seeking a solution to the road repair problem the Government passed the Highway Act of 1835. This act allowed the charging of tolls for the use of roads for those using horses or horse-drawn transport. The tolls would (in theory) then be used by a newly established 'turnpike trust' for that locality to maintain and improve the roads in the area. Stretches of roads maintained under this system would have a tollhouse (with a keeper) and a tollgate, the gate being opened to allow passage after the relevant toll had been paid. Toll charges, however, were not limited to simply meeting the cost of repairing and improving the roads; in order to encourage the creation of trusts an element of profit had to be available to those enterprising gentlemen who, almost literally, went down this road. The result was that in the rural areas of Glamorgan and Carmarthen it was said that a man could not ride 100 yards without paying a toll.

The level of profit from the tolls was not controlled by the Government with the result that some trusts charged tolls that produced an income that far surpassed the cost of any work that might be carried out on the roads under its control. Indeed, there were cases where the company running a trust (and the men behind it) prospered, while the roads under its superintendence deteriorated for lack of attention.

It was against this troubled background that civil unrest first appeared in Pembrokeshire in May 1839, when a group of men demolished a toll gate near Narberth. Interestingly, the men were disguised in women's clothing. Further sporadic attacks on toll-gates were carried out in the coming months and years, and included attacks on several workhouses, the stark symbols of the much hated 'new' Poor Law. The unrest peaked in 1843, at which time the local efforts at controlling the disturbances were strength-ened by the Government sending troops and members of the Metropolitan Police to assist. By this time the nature of the attacks had taken on a more violent hue, a far cry from earlier days when a pantomime-type atmosphere seems to have prevailed at some gatherings. Pat Malloy quotes a memorable account of a January 1843 attack on a toll gate in his book *And they Blessed Rebecca* (Gomer Press):

> *It was about midnight . . . when a large crowd, this time all on foot, dressed in a variety of garments, faces blackened, and armed with the usual array of weaponry, walked up to the gate at Pwll Trap. They halted a few yards short, and the lady Rebecca – stooped, hobbling, and leaning like an old woman on 'her' blackthorn stick – walked up to the gate. Her sight apparently failing her, she reached out with her staff and touched it. 'Children' she said, 'there is something put up here; I cannot go on.' 'What is it mother?' cried her daughters. 'Nothing should stop your way.' Rebecca, peering at the gate, replied 'I do not know children. I am old and cannot see well.' 'Shall we come on mother and move it out of the way?' 'Stop' said she, 'let me see' and she tapped the gate again with her staff. 'It seems like a great gate put across the road to stop your old mother.' whined the old one. 'We will break it mother' her daughters cried in unison; 'nothing shall hinder you on your journey.' 'No,' she persisted, 'let us see; perhaps it will open.' She felt the lock, as would one who was blind. 'No children, it is bolted and locked and I cannot go on. What is to be done?' 'It must be taken down mother, because you and your children must pass.' . . . Rebecca's reply came loud and clear: 'Off with it then my dear children. It has no business here.' And within ten minutes the gate was chopped to pieces and the 'family' had vanished into the night.*

Rebecca Rioters attacking a toll gate. Mary Evans Picture Library

The reference to 'Rebecca' has a biblical origin – Genesis (chapter 24, verse 60) states:

And they blessed Rebecca and said unto her, Thou art our sister, be thou the mother of thousands of millions and let thy seed possess the gates of those who hate them.

Several bands of Rebecca's followers periodically roamed the countryside at this time and each would be led by a 'woman' called Rebecca who rode a white horse to help identify 'her' as the leader. This was a fact that did not escape the attention of the authorities when attempting to make arrests. All the men were dressed in women's clothing, typically an outlandish mix of dresses and hats, with their faces frequently blackened. Such behavior added to the idea of a host of almost 'avenging angels' standing up for the poor and oppressed. Such dress also helped disguise the identities of the protagonists, who would return to their everyday activities in between the odd spot of gate-breaking and arson.

So it was in September 1843 that Messrs Llewelyn and Dillwyn, Mr Moggridge and Mr Peake, Captain Napier and six policemen waited patiently in a damp field near Pontarddulais for events to

Lewis Llewelyn Dillwyn in the 1860s. He was the younger brother of John Dillwyn Llewelyn. John had had to add the 'Llewelyn' to his surname to meet the terms of an inheritance. The Penllergare Trust

unfold. It was now around midnight and the fields were partly illuminated by the light of a glowing moon. It soon became apparent that some sort of procession was under way in the vicinity of Pontarddulais. The sound of gunfire reached the ears of the huddled group, as did the noise of numerous horns being blown. Rockets were observed in the sky, there was much shouting and the sound of many horses' hooves. Added to this cacophony of sound was a noise that sounded like the mewing of cats or high-pitched women's voices. Also heard was a call of 'Come, come' that was repeated three times. This in turn was followed by a shout of 'Gate, gate' presumably as the mob's intended target came into view.

Lewis Llewelyn Dillwyn kept a keen eye on an inn that stood on the other side of the Pontarddulais Bridge and was kept by Mr Griffith Vaughan. Dillwyn saw the flashes and noise of a number of guns being discharged in the vicinity of the inn, promptly followed by a great amount of discordant noise. It was apparent that the noise and its creators were approaching the tollgate. Having reached their apparent objective the assembled throng noisily discharged their guns once again and this was followed by the sound of timber being chopped and hammered. The destruction of the tollgate was underway. It was now 12.45 am.

Charles Frederick Napier, Chief Constable of Glamorgan in 1843. Recklessly brave, he won the respect of all who knew him. South Wales Police Museum

Chief Constable Napier, a hardened veteran of the Rifle Brigade and apparently fearless, quickly took decisive action, despite the numerical inferiority of his party. He ordered his small group to move onto the road and, with this accomplished, they all ran while stooping below the height of a roadside hedge towards the gate, which was about 150 yards away. As they neared the tollgate they observed, for the first time, a band of men, well over a 100 strong, some mounted and some on foot, who were busily engaged in the destruction of the gate as well as its attendant tollgate house. Though obviously men, they were dressed as women, wearing a mix of dresses and bonnets, while some had their coats turned round. Rebecca was clearly at her destructive work. Captain Napier called out in a loud voice that the men were to desist immediately from their criminal actions.

The response from the mass of men was almost instantaneous; a man on a white horse (or possibly a horse draped in a white sheet) wheeled towards Napier's party and rode straight at them, attempting, so it seemed, to run over them with the horse's hooves. At this Dillwyn, far removed from his grand house at Parcwern or his comfortable seat in the magistrates court at Swansea, calmly drew his flintlock pistol. Aiming for the fast moving horse – a larger target then the rider – he was dismayed to find the gun misfire. At the same time he became aware of a ragged volley of shots which he believed had come from the followers of Rebecca and were aimed at the forces of law and order. This volley was met with a more disciplined reply in kind by the small band of police and civilians. Clearly, there was to be no 'pantomime' performance by Rebecca on this night.

Dillwyn managed to avoid the charge of the onrushing horse and rider while at the same time attempting to discharge his other pistol – which also misfired. Though it was of no consolation whatsoever to him at so desperate a time, he concluded that creeping about in wet fields had dampened his gunpowder. If this was not bad enough he now found himself the target of another horse and rider. Drawing a small detonating pistol he managed to fire it into the horses' side at close range and saw the horse stagger as it passed him (he learned that it had died soon afterwards, and that the rider had later been wounded and captured).

With a spirited melee now in progress around him Dillwyn was passed by another rioter who was on foot and apparently keen to make good his escape. Dillwyn grabbed the man as he passed only for him to respond by swinging a large wooden stake at the magistrate's head. Parrying the blow and wrenching the stake off the man, Dillwyn returned the compliment by breaking the stake over the man's head, so that he momentarily slumped into a hedge. The man was not finished, however, and on regaining his feet he continued to grapple with Dillwyn before finally breaking free, pursued by the determined magistrate who managed to land several more blows with what was left of the stake. Several shots were aimed at the man by police officers as he fled, before he was finally overpowered by several policemen who eventually hand-cuffed him to another prisoner. With things not going their way the

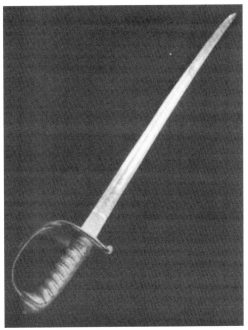

A Glamorgan police jacket from 1841. A 'stove-pipe' hat would also be worn, giving the wearer an imposing presence (left). A police sword, marked 'Rifle Brigade' it might have belonged to the Glamorgan Chief Constable Napier. Though the police usually had only a truncheon, a cutlass or pistol might be carried where real trouble was anticipated (right). South Wales Police Museum

rest of the mob started to make their hasty getaways and retreated over the bridge in great confusion.

Captain Napier meanwhile had been engaged in a tussle with Rebecca 'herself'. Having been shot at by the mob leader, Napier had told his men to 'Mark that man' before bringing the horse and rider down with a shot of his own. He was still struggling with the man when he was struck on the back of the head by an unidentified assailant, rendering him temporarily unconscious. At this point, seeing his captain in trouble, Sergeant Jenkins shot Rebecca, striking him in the arm. Though the wounded man attempted to escape over the river bridge he was apprehended by Police Constable John Price and placed under arrest.

The prisoners, of which there were three (two of them wounded), including the present incarnation of Rebecca herself, were then moved temporarily into what was left of the tollhouse, the doors and windows having been smashed in, as well as the internal woodwork destroyed. Some stones had also been worked out of a wall before the work was interrupted.

Fearing that the routed rioters might regroup and return to attempt to free the prisoners, a messenger was dispatched to Swansea with an urgent request that the Dragoons based at Swansea be brought up as soon as possible. These troops arrived soon afterwards and were shortly followed by a body of the 76th Infantry which had come up from Llanelli. The prisoners were then taken into Swansea in a Phaeton carriage which had been handily provided by the landlord of the nearby inn, with an escort of Dragoons. Dillwyn then walked to Mr Llewelyn's residence at Penllergare, before taking his gig (which he had left there earlier) to his home at Parcwern. Several other prisoners who had been captured by Chambers' party on the Carmarthen side of the bridge were taken to Llanelli to face the magistrates there.

Napier's prisoners were treated for their wounds at Swansea where it was discovered that 'Rebecca' was actually John Hughes of Ty Isha, the son of a farmer residing in the hamlet of Llanon, near Llanelli. Hughes had received a gunshot wound in the left arm, on the outside of the elbow joint after escaping from Napier's grasp. The ball had flattened during its progress in his body and had shattered a bone in the arm. It seemed likely that the arm could not be saved. He also had a wound to the head. In his pocket were found a quantity of percussion caps and powder, about three shillings in cash and a notice which read:

> *Daniel Jones, of Brynhir – Come with all to assist to Jac Ty Isha Wednesday night next; or you will have no further notice – Becca.*

The other wounded man – who had wrestled with Lewis Llewelyn Dillwyn – was David Jones, who had the misfortune to be accidentally hit in the back with small shot known to have been fired by his comrades, as neither the police nor the magistrates were using such weapons. He was described as being in a precarious state. A third man – John Hugh – was less sorely wounded and was put in a prison cell rather than the infirmary.

If the authorities felt that there was some justification for a celebration for having captured at least one ring-leader of the Rebecca gangs such sentiments proved to be decidedly short-lived. On the following Saturday it was the turn of the toll gate at Hendy, near Pontarddulais, to be the target of the rioters. And on this occasion there would be a fatality.

The Hendy tollgate was controlled by Sarah Williams, a woman who was over seventy years of age. Though she had only occupied this position for a week or so, she was, in fact, a very experienced – and very unpopular – collector of tolls. It was rumoured locally that she had been put in at Hendy with the sole aim of increasing the tolls collected due to her known determination to let no one pass without paying. This had led in turn to several anonymous warnings being given to her about the potential danger to her personal safety as a result of her role. These threats she chose to ignore with tragic consequences.

At about 1.00 am on the morning of Saturday, 9 September 1843, Rebecca and her followers came to make good their threats about the Hendy toll gate. Awoken by the sound of hammering on the door of the tollhouse Sarah Williams was confronted by a small number of men, their faces blackened and wearing the now familiar disguises. Pushing past her they quickly emptied the house of her belongings before throwing flaming torches into the small, two roomed building. The thatched roof soon caught fire and as the building blazed in front of the horrified tollgate keeper, several guns were discharged in the air.

Near neighbours John and Margaret Thomas at first decided that discretion was most definitely the better part of valour and remained indoors until Sarah Williams pounded on their door. She begged them to help her save her belongings which were dangerously close to the fire. Mrs Thomas relented of her earlier caution and helped drag some items away from the fire before returning to the relative safety of her own home. She was unable to persuade the distraught Williams to come with her, however. After a while the sound of gunfire lessened and the flames burnt less fiercely. It seemed that, with her task accomplished, Rebecca was slowly bidding her farewell to the smouldering scene of devastation.

The Thomas's still cowered inside their house when they became aware of a strange sound outside. Cautiously peering out they discovered Sarah Williams, slowly crawling alongside the wall of their house, her forehead bloodied and her face stained by smoke from the fire. Helping her quickly inside they had hardly settled her down when the old woman expired. It seemed that Rebecca, notorious for the destruction of property, had not baulked at the destruction of a human life on this occasion.

On the following morning local medical men Mr Benjamin Thomas and Mr John Kirkhouse Cook, both from Llanelli, examined the body which was now lying at the *Black Horse Inn* at Pontarddulais. Thomas told the coroner's inquest that whilst marks of violence were not obviously visible on the body they were nevertheless present. He referred to the marks of small shots which had penetrated the nipple of the left breast and several shots that had struck the arms of the deceased. One shot had struck the windpipe and several more the forehead. More shots had struck the head but had not pierced the skull whilst others were found to have entered a lung, which had subsequently filled with about three pints of blood. On moving the body into an upright position a large quantity of blood escaped from the mouth.

Mr Cook confirmed the observations of his colleague, adding that the loss of blood into the lungs and chest would have hampered breathing whilst the amount of blood lost would in itself be enough to bring on death. There was no other cause that could be responsible for the blood loss other than the shots which had struck the unfortunate Sarah Williams.

The modern-day Black Horse Inn *at Pontarddulais. Sarah Williams' body was conveyed there after her death.* The author

The evidence having been concluded, the coroner asked the jury to retire and consider its verdict, in what must have seemed to be an open and shut case. Whilst no suspects were in custody a verdict of willful murder by person or persons unknown would be enough to allow the bringing of a murder charge at a future trial, assuming the culprits could be eventually apprehended. At the very least a finding of manslaughter – assuming an assailant, if or when apprehended, claimed to have acted in self defence – would be anticipated. After an expectedly brief retirement the jury returned its verdict which was, by contrast, entirely unexpected. It stated:

That the deceased died from an effusion of blood into the chest, which occasioned suffocation – but from what cause is to this jury unknown.

It is likely that several factors caused the jury to return what seemed so perverse a verdict based on the facts placed before it. Local feeling was that Sarah Williams was unpopular due to her chosen work and had been foolish to place herself in harm's way when Rebecca called. Why did not the silly old woman simply run away until the deed was done and the gate destroyed? The toll-gates and their unscrupulous owners were also unpopular while Rebecca and her followers were viewed sympathetically by some as striking back on behalf of the local population, who all felt the sting of the tolls as they went about their daily business.

Why would Rebecca have killed a harmless, if unpopular, old woman? Some suspected that she had recognized one or more of the gang and as such had to be silenced. Others believed that it had simply been a tragic accident. An old woman running about as her house blazed and excitable men fired guns for effect represented a clearly dangerous situation. Could she not have simply crossed into the path of a gun loaded with small shot just as it was randomly aimed and fired? In any event, no charges were pressed against any suspects and the matter was effectively closed.

Awaiting his trial for the earlier attack on the gate at Pontard-dulais, John Hughes might have pondered whether the local sympathy for the rioters shown at the inquest on Sarah Williams might also work in his favour. However, as it became apparent to the Government that local empathy with the rioters was apparently distorting the course of justice, so a decision was made to move the trial of John Hughes away from his own locality and up to Cardiff. The trial was not to be held under the usual Assize system but

A memorial stone to Sarah Williams at Pontarddulais. Sarah was killed during the attack on the Hendy Tollgate in 1843. The date on the stone should read 9 September 1843. The author

was instead convened under Her Majesty's Commission of Oyer and Terminer ('hear and determine'), which established a special commission, outside of the usual law courts, to enquire into the recent disturbances in South Wales and determine the guilt or innocence of any accused. The commission was held at Cardiff and commenced in October 1843. Mr Baron Gurney presided and he was assisted by Mr Justice Cresswell. The Attorney General and Solicitor, assisted by several eminent lawyers, presented the case for the Crown, while the defence was led by Mr Mathew Davenport Hill.

Hill, of course, faced an immediate difficulty; his clients had been caught red handed at the scene of the alleged crimes and two of them had been wounded in the affray. His opening ploy was to call into question the make-up of the jury. This had been chosen, as was the custom, by the High Sheriff of Glamorgan, Mr John Homfray. Hill contended that this gentleman had not acted in an impartial manner when selecting names from those eligible to serve, but he was unable to produce any evidence in support of his allegation. Subsequently his proposition failed. With the prosecution duly producing copious incriminating evidence from the magistrates and police officers who had taken part in the affair, Hill's next gambit was to challenge the accuracy of the actual indictments.

The charges faced by the defendants were that of riotous assembly; that they had begun to demolish the tollgate house; and that they had fired at the chief constable and the other police officers. In the numerous affadavits of interested parties the toll-gate house had variously been described as the 'dwelling house' of William Lewis (the toll collector), Mr Thomas Bullin (a notorious 'toll farmer' to whom Lewis paid the tolls) or the turnpike road trustees. Whilst it was clearly not the home of Bullin or the trustees Hill also noted that Lewis was only a tenant. He argued that the Crown was required to produce 'best evidence' and in that case the trustees should have been called to give evidence rather than Lewis, who was a mere servant. Regrettably for Hill (and his clients) the prosecution was able to muster enough case precedents to demolish his argument in a more thorough manner than had befallen the tollhouse itself. Desperate attempts by Hill to throw doubts on the evidence of identification of the offenders also largely foundered.

Hill then switched his attack to the police use of firearms. Police evidence was mixed on this point. Captain Napier could not recall giving any order for his men to fire. Police Constable George Jones stated that the order to fire had come from Captain Napier whilst Constable Thomas Jones recalled no such command, adding that the police – who were not usually armed – in any event had no set command for such a circumstance as firing on an armed mob. A pragmatic Jones stated that he had simply fired on the mob after the mob had fired on him.

Hill also asked the jury to consider why the police had gone out, armed with pistols loaded with deadly musket balls, to face a mob who only fired small shot and then, often only for dramatic effect. The paramount duty of the police was to protect the innocent, not punish the guilty stated Hill. Being forewarned of the impending attack on the tollgate why had action not been taken by the police to prevent it rather than wait until it was underway before responding? He could not recall a prosecution where those who fled were in the dock while the attackers gave evidence for the prosecution.

The Baron Gurney then summed up the evidence before the jury retired to consider the competing arguments and arrive at a decision. After only thirty minutes a tap on the door of the jury room indicated that matters were coming to a head. With the jury having been ushered back to their places the foreman was asked whether John Hughes was guilty of riotous assembly to which the response was 'guilty'. Similarly to the charges of partly demolishing the tollhouse and firing at the police, the verdict was again 'guilty', but with a strong recommendation for mercy on account of Hughes's previous good character. Sentence was then deferred as the two other defendants had yet to be dealt with.

Monday, 30 October 1843 was the day that the trial of David Jones and John Hugh was due to begin. When placed in the dock and asked how they pleaded both responded 'not guilty'. However, the decision in Hughes's case must have made an impression, and after some whispered conversations with their legal advisers the question was put to them again. This time both men pleaded 'guilty'. Mr Hill rose to say that he hoped that their obvious penitence would be taken into account when sentence was passed. He went on to say that the three men had already suffered harsh treatment in prison as a result of their having scuffled with the police at Pontarddulais. Additionally, Hughes had suffered a permanent disability to his arm while David Jones still had several slugs in his body that could not be safely removed. All three were of hitherto good character.

Mr Baron Gurney then proceeded to pass sentence noting that the three men stood:

> *... convicted of a felony of a very exaggerated description, in that you banded and associated with others, who assembled in great number, in the dead of night, armed with deadly weapons, and were not indisposed to use them ... For the purpose of vindicating that law which you have offended, great, and I hope salutary, examples must be made.*

Gurney went on to note that each man was liable to transportation for life for the crime for which he stood convicted. However, taking into account all mitigating factors, he felt able to reduce that sentence in the cases of David Jones and John Hugh to a period of seven years. He saw little in the way of redeeming features in the case of John Hughes, however. He regarded Hughes as being from a '... different station in society ...' As such he should not have been led astray by others and should certainly not have been an instigator and ringleader in his own right. The papers found on his person – some of which were threatening in nature – cast his case in a different light to that of the other defendants. On that basis the sentence for John Hughes would be transportation for twenty years.

The sentences were duly carried out in March 1844 when the prisoners were embarked onto the *London*, arriving at Maria Island (off the coast of Van Diemen's Land, modern day Tasmania) in July 1844. A week after arrival David Jones died. He was only twenty-one years of age. We can only wonder whether his untimely death was due to the bullets that remained in his body or perhaps it was a disease contracted on the voyage. Who is to say that one so young, when separated from all he had known and loved, did not simply die of grief? John Hugh remained on the island and was freed in December 1850, having completed his sentence. In 1852 he was recorded as requesting permission to marry another convict, the wife he had left behind in Carmarthenshire having presumably died in the meantime.

At the time of his transportation John Hughes had never before seen a packet steamer or a train, and he showed great curiosity in his surroundings as he was transported to the Millbank Prison at London, prior to embarkation. Though he had expressed a wish to return home at some time he actually remained in Tasmania until his death about the year 1900. He had been granted a conditional pardon with just over six years of his sentence still remaining. In 1864 he was working as a timber cutter and employed men to assist him in that enterprise. He was then writing in English, having apparently forgotten most of his Welsh, and he kept up a correspondence with his family back in Wales up to the time of his death.

The Rebecca Riots effectively petered out in late 1843 though even in their final year there were over 250 attacks on tollgates in West Wales. Government led attempts to quell the unrest had been largely unsuccessful causing a *Times* reporter to note that in July 1843:

> ... *A detachment of artillery are marching by way of Brecon; a detachment of artillery are marching to Carmarthen by way of Swansea; the whole of the 4th Regiment of Light Dragoons are to be stationed in South Wales; three companies of the 75th Foot are to arrive in Carmarthen within the next two days; the Yeomanry are kept on permanent duty, and every military appliance of the government is exercised, yet not a single outrage has been stayed nor a single Rebeccaite captured ...*

It was people like the undoubtedly brave (some would say reckless) Captain Napier and his men, often acting on paid tip offs, who had the greater success in capturing some of the rioters than the military forces that were deployed. Longer lasting success came in the form of a Royal Commission, set up by the Home Secretary, to inquire into what it was that had caused so much unrest among the rural population of South West Wales. The Commission reported in March 1844 and listed a catalogue of mismanagement by the turnpike trusts and its employees.

Corrective legislation to reform the trusts was drafted and became law in August 1844, at a stroke removing many of the grievances that had hitherto been left to fester unaddressed. Within several years of the reforms it was claimed that the roads in Wales were at least the equal of the best in Britain.

This would have been of little consolation to the numerous captured rioters who were condemned to mark their time on the other side of the world. But there can be no doubt that the actions of the rioters finally spurred the authorities to consider remedial

R·EBEC·A

Dinistriwyd Gât
Pontarddulais
gan Ferched
Beca dan eu harweinydd
John Hughes (Jac Tŷ-isha)
ar Fedi 6ed 1843.

The Pontarddulais
Toll-gate
was destroyed on the
6th September 1843
by the Daughters of
Rebecca led by
John Hughes (Jac Tŷ-isha).

A memorial stone to 'Rebecca' (in this instance John Hughes) who led an attack on the Pontarddulais Tollgate only to be wounded, captured and transported for twenty years. He never returned to his homeland. The author

measures that would otherwise not have been taken, and from that viewpoint their destructive campaign was a success. One other thing is certain: over 160 years after the events took place the rioters are still rightly held in high esteem in the collective memory of communities like Pontarddulais and numerous other towns and villages in South West Wales.

CHAPTER 5

The Fighting Irish and Two Dead Welshmen
1848

Boys! Come out and save me!

On the night of the 8 May 1848 a 'Cwrw Bach' ('small beer') was held in a small court at a thatched cottage called Ty-Wyth on the Carmarthen Road on the outskirts of Swansea. A Cwrw Bach was an unlicensed drinking party where those attending would bring their own beer, frequently home brewed, and then enjoy a night of drinking and carousing with like-minded persons. They were regarded as troublesome hot spots by those in authority in the town. Indeed, in 1845 the chief constable of the Swansea police force had commented that on one occasion he had found several of these events being held simultaneously, with more than 400 persons in all, in attendance.

In the area that night were five Irish labourers who had been engaged in digging out a railway cutting at nearby Loughor. They were now looking for a thirst-quenching drink and some work for the coming days, having just been paid off. They stopped at the *Trap* public house and drank several quarts of beer before being refused any more due to the lateness of the hour. Having walked towards Swansea they came across the *Marquis Arms* where they were also refused any drink. Moving on they encountered Mary Bowen who promised to take them to a venue where getting a late night drink would present no difficulties. Bowen then led them to the cottage where the Cwrw Bach was in full flow. Almost twenty people were in the cottage, several of them in various states of inebriation.

Sitting inside the cottage were John Williams and a man named Pillinger. Williams was engaged in railway work and had the authority to hire men as necessary and was known to at least one of the five Irishmen – Patrick Leary – who immediately approached him and asked about the possibility of work. Williams seemed to not understand the question while Pillinger asked why the Irishman had not phrased it in Welsh. Leary carefully repeated the question in his best Welsh and was told by Williams to attend on him the next day when he might have some work for him. He was told that the daily pay would be 2s 8d a day, which was below the going rate, but Leary was a little desperate for funds so he signalled his reluctant agreement.

Leary then returned to his workmates and was told by one of them, John Norris, to get the beer jug refilled. Leary soon returned with the brimming jug to the cottage kitchen and prepared to take his first swig of beer since his arrival at the Cwrw Bach. However, before he had had a chance to sip it he was accosted by a Welshman who was unknown to him. This man – Edward Morgan, who was drunk – demanded to know why it was that Leary was prepared to work on 'the cheap', when he himself had stopped working for John Williams precisely for that reason, as a matter of principle. The implication was clear – Leary was being accused of undercutting the local supply of labour to the detriment of people like Edward Morgan. Without further ado Morgan grabbed hold of Leary and the two men grappled momentarily and then fell out of the cottage door into the courtyard before Leary was unceremoniously dumped onto the ground. He called out 'Boys! Come out and save me!' to summon the help of his friends.

At the nearby *Marquis Arms* the commotion caught the attention of Mrs Ruth Evans, the landlady of the inn. She summoned her husband and father in law, Mr Jenkin Evans, and, intrigued by the noise, the trio set off in its direction to investigate.

After Leary's call for help it was in fact several Welshmen who first appeared in the yard and these included John Williams, his prospective employer. Leary's call had not been in vain, however, and soon the yard became congested as his fellow Irishmen John Norris, Thomas Martin and Mike Leary (Patrick's brother) all crowded in. To Leary's alarm Tom Martin was not waving his fists but rather a knife which, without a word being spoken, he plunged into the body of John Williams.

In the meantime Mike Leary was wielding his navvies shovel on several Welshmen. Appalled and frightened by what he had witnessed Patrick Leary ran out of the melee and into the road and there he encountered another Welshman who grabbed hold of him and tried to prevent his escape. A shouted voice from the yard indicated – apparently mistakenly – that it was Patrick Leary who had used the knife and this probably stiffened the Welshman's resolve to hold on to his captive.

Another Irishman – William Norris – then appeared in the road and tried to wrest Patrick Leary free from the grip of his captor. He was still trying to do this when Mike Leary arrived and shouted that his brother should be immediately released. When Patrick's captor refused, Mike Leary struck him hard on the head with his shovel. This understandably did the trick and thus freed, Patrick Leary ran off in the direction of Swansea. At this time Mrs Evans, landlady of the *Marquis Arms*, arrived to see several men standing over and beating her father in law, Jenkin Evans, who had left the pub to investigate the disturbance, and who now lay in the road. Several shovel blows were delivered prompting Mrs Evans to scream 'Murder!' In the nearby courtyard lay John Williams, a pool of blood slowly spreading around his body.

As Patrick Leary ran off he heard Billy Norris implore Patrick's brother Mike – who was still actively using his shovel as a weapon – not to leave him. Patrick was soon joined on the run by Thomas Martin who told him that the rest of the gang were on the way. The two men paused breathlessly at the Cwmbwrla gate near Swansea and there Martin confided in Leary that during the scuffle he was '. . . the boy that let the wind pass through some of them . . .' Leary and Martin then reached Swansea where Leary stayed overnight at a lodging house he frequented next to the Bethesda Chapel.

Leary heard the following morning that two men were dead following the previous night's brawl and he quickly gathered together his sparse belongings and took to the road. His four fellow countrymen did likewise. None of them got very far; local magistrate John Dillwyn Llewelyn was indefatigable in his exertions to bring the offenders to justice. Thomas Martin hid at the Red Jacket quarry near Briton Ferry but was discovered by some of the workmen. Making a further dash for freedom he was later found hiding in a bush and given over to the custody of Police Constable John Price of Neath. He was later transferred to Swansea. Police Sergeant John Price (John Price being a popular name amongst policemen of the time, apparently) and Thomas Gray set out from Swansea in disguise, having been given some information on the whereabouts of the other four.

When about three miles outside Cowbridge they espied four men walking along one of whom was definitely identified as Patrick

John Dillwyn Llewelyn in the early 1850s. Magistrates were often on 'the front line' at this time, being required to literally 'read the Riot Act' to angry crowds. The Penllergare Trust

Leary by Thomas Gray, who knew him by sight. They overtook the group, stopped at a nearby inn, and alerted the landlord to their purpose. When the four reappeared they had spread out a little along the road and this allowed Sergeant Price to allow some of the group to pass before he arrested Patrick Leary and lodged him temporarily in the care of the landlord. On catching up with the other men Gray was able to confirm that they were not the men sought. Price and Gray then duly completed their walk to

Cowbridge where, in a situation often complained about to the present day, the expected local police constable could not at first be found.

Eventually reinforced by the initially scarce local constable they simply waited until a group of men in navvies garb could be seen approaching the town hall. Gray was then able to confirm that the three innocent men seen earlier had subsequently been joined on the walk by the three men who were being still sought by the police. The three suspects were immediately arrested in the presence of several local citizens who gave what assistance they could. They seemed much dejected and offered no resistance. They were later moved to Swansea where a crowd of several thousand greeted them with insults and threats, such was the feeling in the town following the double murder.

At the coroner's inquest into the deaths of John Williams (aged forty-seven) and Jenkin Evans (aged fifty-two) medical evidence was given by Mr W H Michael, surgeon, and Dr George Gwynne Bird. It was reported that there were no marks of violence on the body of Williams except for an incised wound on the left breast below the nipple. This was an inch and a half long and had penetrated between the fifth and sixth ribs. It had then damaged

Police handcuffs. These were locked by use of a screw key. The smaller-wristed set shown was for use on children. South Wales Police Museum

the lower part of the left lung and passed on to similarly strike the heart. The left ventricle had been pierced and the left cavity of the chest was filled with blood, as was the pericardium. Both men agreed that this wound was the cause of death, which would have swiftly followed.

In the case of Jenkin Evans the medical evidence revealed a similar pattern; there was a small would on the left hand side of the chest. On post mortem this was found to have penetrated a large vein that was known as the *vena cava* and led to the heart. That being the case, death would have been almost instantaneous opined the learned medical men. It was also stated that the wounds could have been produced by the same instrument – probably a knife – though that was not a certainty.

Having heard the evidence of witnesses, doctors and testimony from some of those apprehended in connection with the crime, the inquest jury returned verdicts of wilful murder in both cases, with Thomas Martin being accused of the death of John Williams and Michael Leary being accused in the case of Jenkin Evans. John Norris was adjudged to have provided material assistance to the perpetrators. As a rider the jury requested that the authorities should take firm action to put a stop to '. . . the unlawful and abominable meetings termed "Cwrw Bach" . . .'. The three men were then remanded to await trial at the next assizes.

The trial took place in the third week of July 1848. No true bill was found against John Norris and he was therefore discharged. Representing the Crown against Martin and Michael Leary were Messrs W R Grove and Mr Benson, while the defence was conducted by Mr Sergeant Jones and Mr Albert Jenkin. Both men were charged with the wilful murder of John Williams.

Patrick Leary was called to give evidence and it is hard not to wonder how his evidence was affected by the fact that his brother was one of the accused. Patrick recalled having seen Thomas Martin stooping down near the *Beaufort Arms* and sharpening a knife on a stone. He described it as being a large pocket knife, about five inches long. Leary also stated that he had seen Martin use the knife at work for various purposes. As regards the brawl at the cwrw bach Patrick Leary accepted that he had been involved in the scuffle and testified that he had seen Martin holding his knife and striking John Williams with it. Williams immediately fell to the floor and did not subsequently utter a word.

Mr Sergeant Jones, for the defence, tried to show that there had been bad blood over work issues between Patrick Leary and Thomas Martin prior to the brawl at the cwrw bach. Jones also questioned whether there was historic animosity between Cork men and Tipperary men, Leary being from Cork, while Martin was from Tipperary. Whether these factors might flavour Leary's evidence to the detriment of his client was the subtly stated accusation. If he could put doubt in the minds of the jurors on those points it might throw Leary's evidence into doubt as he would be seen to be implicating a man he was at loggerheads with. The next witness, William Norris, another of the Irish contingent, said that he had seen Michael Leary with a knife on the day of the murder though he added that it was a shovel that he had seen Michael use as a weapon in the yard. As Jones then showed, no doubt hoping the jury also took heed, Norris was also a Cork man. Could his evidence be fully relied on against someone from Tipperary?

Another witness confirmed that Martin had a knife that he kept sharpened while William Goodenough testified that Martin had recently threatened to stab a workmate. When challenged at work by Goodenough about his cavalier attitude to the use of his knife Martin had threatened to run it into him as well. Martin claimed that his knife had never left his pocket; he was being framed by the other Irishmen, most of whom he barely knew.

Police Sergeant John Price had apprehended four of the navvies (Martin excepted) near Cowbridge. He confirmed that spots found on a coat owned by Michael Leary had been determined by the medical experts, Michael and Bird, to be blood. Leary was also in possession of a knife at the time of his capture. Sergeant Price also recounted conversations he had overheard between his captives. Michael Leary had said 'We shall all be hung', adding later that if he were to be hung for this it would not be for the first. This was important evidence. Was Michael Leary tacitly admitting that if he were hung it would be for the death of Jenkin Evans rather than John Williams who was the first man struck? And, in the confusion in the courtyard, had he found time to draw his knife unobserved after first using his shovel as a weapon on the helpless Jenkin Evans? Leary had later claimed that he had meant that he would not be the first man hung on a mistaken finding of guilty.

With the prosecution case concluded Mr Sergeant Jones delivered what was described as an able and very impressive speech. Indeed, he took almost two hours in going over the salient points and reaping the maximum benefit for his clients. He abhorred the prevalence of the cwrw bach meetings in the locality. His clients had attended the one at Fforestfach but there could be no doubt that they did so to slake their thirsts rather than to engage in any violent skulduggery. There was no element of premeditation whatsoever.

Jones then went on to cast doubt on the evidence of Patrick Leary. His account of events was improbable according to Mr Sergeant Jones. After all he was the instigator of the original affray. If he had only been involved in a minor scuffle in the yard why did he then find it necessary to flee the scene and, indeed, the town unless he was not as innocent as his evidence suggested? Jones felt that it was on the evidence of Patrick Leary that the Crown case stood or fell. He trusted that the jury would realise that he was as much mixed up in the tragic affair as the prisoners at the bar and as such his evidence must be treated with the utmost caution.

His attention then turned to the evidence of the policemen. He cautioned the jury that the police, due to their frequent dealings with thieves and the like, could be a little too eager to get successful prosecutions. This could lead to mistakes, no doubt genuine, on their part in later recalling what was supposed to have been said by those apprehended. Words, after all, were 'as fleet as the wind'. Had Price actually heard what he said he heard? Or did he think he heard what he wanted to hear? He concluded by reminding the jury that it was Patrick's brother Michael who stood in the dock and that animosity traditionally existed between gentlemen from Cork and Tipperary. These factors might have played a part in Patrick Leary's evidence against Thomas Martin. The doubts so raised were quite explicit and must pose a reasonable doubt as to exactly who had done what argued the defence. On that basis the jury must acquit both men contended Mr Sergeant Jones.

The judge then proceeded to sum up for the jury. He expressed surprise that despite John Williams having been stabbed to death while in a crowded courtyard only one man, Patrick Leary, had observed the deed. If the jury were persuaded that one of the accused had indeed struck the fatal blow then the next question was whether they considered that both of the accused men were set on a common course to resist all interference with their aim, even to the death. If that was their common design then both men were guilty, irrespective of who struck the fatal blow.

In a step by step exposition the learned judge then addressed the difference between murder and manslaughter for the benefit of the jury. He stated that in all cases of homicide the first presumption was that it amounted to murder. This presumption was strengthened where the attack, as in the present case, involved a deadly weapon, such as a knife. Nothing but the most extreme necessity would justify the use of such a weapon in self-defence. The evidence, as presented, seemed to support Patrick Leary's contention that Martin had inflicted the fatal wound. But did he do it while being aided and abetted by Michael Leary? If that was Michael Leary's role then he too was guilty of murder despite his not having struck the blow. Patrick Leary's evidence on this point was critical; but could he be trusted? Only the jury could decide on these issues and that was a momentous burden for its members.

After deliberating for only fifteen minutes the jury returned to deliver a verdict of 'guilty' of murder against both Thomas Martin and Michael Leary. This apparently unexpected decision produced a marked sensation in the previously hushed court, though the convicted men displayed no visible signs of emotion. Silence was restored when the judge put on the dreaded black cap and addressed the prisoners. He expressed agreement with the verdict of the jury and criticised the demeanour of the duo during the trial. This, he thought, showed that they were both hardened to an incredible degree. He added:

> *By law, both human and divine, you have incurred the terrible penalty of death. There is, I fear, on earth no hope for you. Let me therefore most earnestly and solemnly entreat you to make the best use you can of the short period which remains for you in this world, and by earnest prayer and sincere repentance endeavour to make peace with your creator, and obtain in Heaven that mercy which will be denied you on earth . . .*

He then proceeded to pronounce sentence of death in the usual form. The prisoners appeared to remain unmoved by their awful plight though Martin did say 'I am as innocent as the child unborn' while Leary stood silently at his side.

News of the verdict spread quickly amongst the Irish community in South Wales. It was met with great anger. At Cardiff, where the trial was held, a threatening crowd had surrounded the chief witness, Patrick Leary, at the end of the case, resulting in numerous scratches to his body before he escaped and sought the shelter of the local police station. Rumours also abounded that Patrick was actually a person of ill repute whose evidence should have been discounted. By contrast Thomas Martin was depicted as a quiet and inoffensive man. Appeals for clemency from citizens in both Swansea and Cardiff were conveyed by Mr Vivian to Sir George Grey in London.

These appeals seem to have met with eventual success. Though the surviving local records are inconclusive it seems that in due course both men were granted 'respite' though whether this means they were acquitted on appeal or simply had their sentences reduced (possibly to transportation) is not stated. One thing is certain: neither man appears in the lists of the hanged so the trial judge's opinion that they would not obtain mercy in this world was proved incorrect.

Chapter 6

A Greek Tragedy:
The Canal Bank Killing
1858

... they had hauled in the body of a man.

I n 1858 Swansea was a thriving port with an international trade in copper, coal and other items. As such it attracted ships from many parts of the world, each with their own crews of differing nationalities. Naturally, the attractions that Swansea had to offer men who had spent long periods at sea were many, and included the usual run of public houses, so-called 'dancing establishments' with a steady supply of willing 'dancing' partners, food shops and cheap lodgings. However, tensions within this international hotchpotch were ever present and occasionally bubbled up into acts of violence.

One such incident occurred on the 16 February 1858. At about 9.00 pm on a cold evening Francis Henwood and Thomas Johns were watching a boat carrying a cargo of tin on the canal just opposite the *Ship and Castle* public house. In the stillness of the night they heard sounds of what seemed to be a nearby scuffle, and raised voices in a foreign tongue. A few minutes later they heard a loud splash, as if something had fallen or been thrown into the canal.

Their curiosity aroused, they determined to investigate what had happened and to this end they made their way along the canal bank, in the direction from whence the sounds had come. By the light of the moon they soon espied a white object floating on the dark waters of the canal, but could not ascertain what it was. Henwood obtained a boat hook which he handed to Johns who, in turn, hooked and then pulled to the side of the canal bank the unidentified bundle. By the dim light of a guttering candle they discovered that they had hauled in the body of a man. Unable to pull the body from the waters themselves they enlisted the assistance of several nearby stable hands and finally got it ashore. The still warm – but quite dead – body produced a trail of vapour in the cold night air.

The police were promptly summoned and Sergeant Neale arrived at the canal side within fifteen minutes of the grim discovery having been made. With the aid of his police lantern Neale observed a serious head wound on the body and confirmed that the man was quite beyond the reach of any aid that might have been offered. Lying on the canal bank was observed a cap, a walking stick, a pipe bowl and a stone.

Some of these items were smeared with blood and, of apparently far greater significance, also found was a lead weight enveloped within a cord wrapping. This was in the style of a sling shot, and suspicion was immediately aroused that this – if swung with considerable force – was the object that had caused the severe head wounds on the victim's body. As the body was placed on a stretcher prior to its conveyance to the *Ship and Castle*, where it would duly receive the attention of the Coroner, a knife fell from the deceased's waist band. A further examination of the body revealed what appeared to be several stab wounds.

Enquiries in the town soon revealed that the deceased man was a Greek cook named Atanasio Mitropanio from the brig *Penelope* which, at that time, was berthed in the float harbour at Swansea. After discussion with the ship's crew the attention of the police was drawn to two Greek sailors who, it was said, were currently lodging at the *Jolly Tar* in Wind Street and had been seen with the deceased on the night in question. Several police officers under the direction of Superintendent Dunn then made their way to the *Jolly Tar*, where they discovered the suspects in an upstairs bedroom where they were immediately apprehended, pending further enquiries. One was named Manoeli Selapatane and a search of his person by Police Constable Noah Owen produced four shillings, five sixpences and four penny pieces in his right hand trouser pocket. The left hand pocket yielded a foreign coin, apparently a Turkish sovereign, a key, a knife and a discharge paper from the last ship on which he had served.

The other prisoner – Panaotis Alepis – was also searched. This revealed three half crowns, twelve shillings, one sixpence, three pence and two half-pence in coinage. Also found were a comb and shoehorn and another discharge certificate [author's note: I have adopted the men's name spellings as shown in an illustration caption in the *Cambrian* newspaper of 19 March 1858; the reported spellings in various newspapers are not consistent and it seems that Alepis also occasionally used an alias]. Selapatane was twenty-eight years old whilst Alepis was twenty-three.

The coroner's inquest was speedily convened under the foremanship of George Grant Francis, who was described as a 'merchant', though he is better known today as a significant historian of Swansea who did much to preserve the town's ancient charters and much more. The Greek gentlemen had the benefit of a translator who had lived in the town for the past three years. The body of the deceased had already been examined by Mr W H Michael, at the request of the coroner.

Mr Michael found the outer coat, shirt and under flannels of the deceased were pierced in several places and these corresponded with the wounds that were visible on the body. Rigor mortis had set in and the face was pale, with the lips almost colourless. Perhaps surprisingly, given the apparent violence directed against the deceased, his expression was tranquil. There were several scratches on the face though these had played no part in the cause of death, having been possibly caused by the fingernails of an assailant.

The hair was matted with blood and it was not until this had been cut away that the true nature of the head injuries became apparent. The scalp was lacerated to a length of five inches on the left side of the head. Several lesser cuts, bruises and contusions were also present. Examination revealed that the skull had been fractured to a length of six inches, with much effusion of blood in the brain cavity. It was likely that the lead weight wrapped in cord was the weapon used to inflict these injuries.

The stab wounds had also been delivered with considerable ferocity. Mr Michael deduced that the implement used must have been a narrow knife or dagger. One stab wound had passed close to the spine, having divided the eighth rib near to the neck and had entered the lung. This was a deep and considerable wound, the blood loss from which had filled the lower part of the lung and infiltrated into the spaces between the larger blood vessels, though the heart remained intact. In Mr Michael's opinion there were several wounds that could have resulted in death; it was impossible to say which had been the prime cause, given the severity of them all. He added that he believed that, owing to the nature and position of the wounds, the deceased man must have been attacked from in front and behind, meaning that two attackers had been involved.

When the facts of the incident were placed under the consideration of George Grant Francis and his jury it took only ten minutes of deliberation before a verdict of wilful murder was returned. The two Greek sailors would soon have to account for their actions before a criminal trial jury, where they would be at risk of a fateful meeting with the public executioner, if their defence did not stand up to a close examination.

In early March 1858 the trial of Manoeli Selapatane and Panaotis Alepis was held at the Glamorgan Assizes. The accused had been provided with Messrs Allen and Rees to argue the case for the defence, as well as the services of an interpreter to assist with translation, neither man being fluent in English. Counsel for the Crown were Messrs Giffard and Bowen, with Mr C B Mansfield, attorney, assisting. Mr Giffard opened the prosecution case by stating that one fact in the case was beyond dispute. That was that the deceased had been hale and hearty only fifteen minutes before his death. He had then had horrific violence meted out to him and the only question was whether it was the men in the dock who had administered the fatal blows. In the absence of modern policing and forensic methods this was open to debate. As the jury would hear there were no direct witnesses to the savage attack and it would be the weight of circumstantial evidence (or lack of it) that would lead the jury to conclude that the right or wrong men were in the dock.

The harrowing details of the discovery of the body and the nature of its injuries were then recounted to the jury before the prosecution called witnesses to try and establish the whereabouts and actions of the accused on the critical night that would put them firmly in the dock as the perpetrators of the evil deed. Called for the prosecution was Mrs Eliza Lovelace, who had provided the accused with lodgings at the *Jolly Tar* on Wind Street. They had arrived on the Friday prior to the murder, which took place on the following Tuesday. On the Tuesday Mrs Lovelace stated that they had left the house between 6.00 and 7.00 pm, returning a little after 9.00 pm and – she thought but was not certain – without their coats on.

Alepis had gone into the rear yard and washed his handkerchief whilst Selapatane had gone straight to their shared bedroom.

However, they did not remain more than ten minutes, at which time they left again, having put on hats and coats that had been left in their room. Mrs Lovelace also confirmed that a hat found at the murder scene was at least very similar to one worn by Selapatane, while a stick found there belonged to Alepis. After leaving the house for a second time the men had returned at around 10.00 pm and gone to bed.

Another witness was George Jafalia who was a crew member on the brig *Penelope*. He had left the deceased, Atanasio Mitropanio, on board the ship at about 6.00 pm. He identified the hat produced by the prosecution as having been worn that evening at a dancing house by the accused, Selapatane. He confirmed that when he had seen the prisoners at the dancing house both had been wearing jackets though these appeared to have been discarded for some reason, prior to their return to Mrs Lovelace and their lodgings at the *Jolly Tar*. The jury was left to ponder whether the jackets had been discarded since they were bloodstained.

Mr Michael, as well as describing the wounds on the body, also confirmed that the items found on the side of the canal were spotted with blood as was a check shirt that had been worn by Alepis at the time of his arrest. Alepis claimed that this had been the result of a nose bleed and, indeed, he suffered a sudden nose bleed during the trial.

Elizabeth Phillips described how she had seen the deceased around the town frequently since his ship came into port. He had frequented the *Powell's Arms*, the 'dancing house' which seemed very popular with visiting seamen. Phillips threw light on the root of its popularity and her probable profession by revealing that he had offered her a sovereign to sleep with him but she had refused. But she had nevertheless kept the sovereign. Behaviour of this sort was probably commonplace in Swansea at this time; a few years later (1865) the Chief Constable reported that in Swansea there were 331 prostitutes, of which six were under sixteen years of age.

Miss Phillips had then met the prisoners between 5.00 and 6.00 pm on the night of the crime and, clearly not being of a shy and retiring nature, she had asked Selapatane if he would partake of a glass of ale with her. With the Greeks apparently short of money Phillips had treated them to a drink in the *Red Lion*, High Street before Selapatane had finally dredged up some small change and was thus able to return the compliment. They warned her that the cook from the *Penelope* would be abroad in disguise that night and she had better not be walking up and down High Street if she wished to avoid trouble. Apparently the fact that she had taken the cook's sovereign but not provided any services in return still rankled with the seaman and he would be looking out for her. A little later that night she had seen the cook, Mitropanio, in the company of Alepis, near the train station at High Street. The couple had then proceeded down High Street towards Wind Street and Phillips never saw the cook again.

Another lady who seemed to enjoy an evening stroll was Elizabeth Thomas, who confirmed that she had seen Alepis and Mitropanio near the train station at about 8.20 pm She was also able to confirm that the plaid cap and stick produced by the prosecution (having been found on the canal bank) were the same that Selapatane had worn in the *Powell's Arms* prior to the murder. Mary Ann Williams stated that she had seen the three men near

Wind Street, Swansea, with the Mackworth Hotel on the right. The Greek sailors proceeded down this street with their victim. West Glamorgan Archive Service

the *Ivorites' Arms* in High Street at about 8.30 pm, at which time they seemed to be exchanging harsh words though the reason for that was unknown.

Thomas Williams was the proprietor of a wax works exhibition that was on display at a High Street premises. He recalled Alepis standing at the door of the exhibition while Mitropanio entered to look at the displays. The cook left after a very cursory inspection, however, and proceeded further down the High Street with Alepis. The witness thought that this was about 8.30 pm on the night of the murder. Another man was standing in the road nearby, but whether this was the second accused man, Williams was not sure.

Frances Maria Edwards and Sarah Lovelace both recalled seeing two men running down the Strand from the area of the canal. Due to the light of a nearby gas street lamp Edwards had got a good look at one of the men – both of whom slowed to a walk when they realised they had been seen – and she was sure that man was Alepis. She also believed that Selapatane was the other man.

At the coroner's inquest Alepis had claimed that he had left the lodging house between 8.00 and 9.00 pm and gone to the dancing house with an unnamed man. They were apparently joined by Selapatane. After this Alepis claimed to have returned to his lodgings, having paused on the way back to buy some bread. Selapatane confirmed some of these details, adding that he had gone to bed before being arrested by the police.

The key factor in a criminal trial of course, be it simple theft or horrific murder, is that the prosecution must prove its case 'beyond a reasonable doubt'. This is a different and sterner test than that employed in the civil courts where a judge may decide a case on the 'balance of probabilities' as outlined in the evidence. The defence in the Alepis-Selapatane case therefore set out to understandably introduce an element (or several) of reasonable doubt into the deliberations of the jury.

Part of the prosecution case was that Elizabeth Phillips had stated that the Greeks were unable to buy her a drink prior to the murder occurring, but that after their arrest they were seen to be in possession of sums of money with an implication that they had robbed their victim. However, it was noted by the defence that Selapatane had in fact purchased drinks prior to the murder, despite earlier saying he had no money. Much was made of the fact that the deceased had been seen at one time to publicly count out his money which included Turkish sovereigns, a coin which had been found on the accused when they were searched. Again, it was noted that it was not uncommon for the Greeks to be paid in such coin, and there was no definite proof that the money held by them had been taken from the deceased.

On the question of the plaid cap and walking stick found abandoned at the murder scene it was observed that similar items were commonplace in the town and there was no testimony that confirmed beyond doubt that the items produced in court had actually belonged to the accused. Additionally while Miss Edwards had testified that she was sure that the men in the dock were the ones who had run past her in the Strand, her friend, Miss Lovelace, was not quite so certain of this fact, and had failed to state categorically that the prisoners were indeed the men she had seen. Was not this apparent uncertainty between people who had witnessed the same scene not enough to cast a doubt in the minds of the jury?

The defence, leaving no angle un-examined, further posed the question that if the accused had not committed the crime then who had? Whilst not wishing or able to point the finger of guilt at any individuals the defence did say that the deceased was well known amongst certain females in the town, who also knew that he routinely had in his possession a large sum of money. Who was to say that one of these persons might not have had the opportunity and the motive to perpetrate a murder in the course of what might have started as a simple robbery? After all no conclusive proof had been introduced to show that the accused had robbed the man and similarly no concrete evidence of a violent argument between the accused and the deceased, ending in horrific violence, had been placed before the jury by the prosecution.

The defence concluded by saying that if the points that had been raised to counter the assertions of the prosecution had raised one iota of doubt in the minds of the jurors then they were duty bound to return a verdict of not guilty.

With both sides having concluded their cases the judge gave a lengthy summing up before asking the jury to retire and consider its verdict. After a retirement of twenty-six minutes the jury returned to the court room and delivered a verdict of 'guilty' on both prisoners. As was customary the guilty men were given the option of saying something before sentence was passed. Alepis stated that he had nothing more to add to his defence and now left his fate in

The Greek sailors, Alepis (left) and Selapatane, await their fate. South West Wales Media. *The Cambrian*

the hands of God. He did enquire though, as to the planned date of his execution.

Selapatane spoke through his interpreter only to say that he was innocent of the crime of which he had been convicted. The judge then passed a sentence of death on both men in the prescribed manner, speaking over Alepis's repeated assertions that he knew nothing of the matter of which he had been convicted. Alepis concluded by adding that the law in England and Wales was very different to that of his own country. Had he been tried in Greece he was certain that he would have been acquitted. The judge, perhaps sensing a little bewilderment on the part of the condemned men, went to some length to emphasise that the sentence that had been passed on them would duly be put into effect. As

such they would be well advised to make their spiritual arrangements accordingly. Suitable ministers of religion would no doubt
be provided on request by the appropriate authorities.

It was later reported that the enormity of what they had done
and what an awful fate awaited them began to weigh heavily on
the condemned men. Their previously indifferent outlook had
departed and they now spent much of their time in reading Greek
scriptural works, provided for them by the Archimandrite of the
Greek Church. This gentleman was also in personal attendance
on them and it seems his exhortations produced a change in attitude though confessions were not forthcoming. Selapatane wrote
a letter home on his own behalf as well as one for his fellow
countryman outlining their coming fate, but still protesting their
innocence.

The date of execution was set for 20 March 1858, little more
than a month after the crime was committed. As the execution was
to be staged in public it attracted a large number of spectators,
many of whom the *Cambrian* newspaper confirmed as being of
the 'lower orders'. Many of these thousands of people, including
'showmen, booths-men, gamblers etc' arrived on the day before
the execution, many of them sped in by the railway. Also present
were labourers, carpenters, engineers and mechanics, together
with women with children in arms, shoeless lads with scanty
tattered clothing and a healthy contingent of what the *Cambrian*
called the 'city Arabs'. The newspaper grudgingly admitted that
some of the '. . . better grade of society . . .' were also drawn to the
spectacle.

On the day of the execution the sun shone brightly and the sky
was clear. The scaffold had been erected on the south west corner
of the prison building, at an angle opposite the infirmary and the
Union poor law house. Every inch of ground was packed with
spectators, some of whom had climbed into trees and onto the
roofs of houses in order to get a better view of the macabre proceedings.

William Calcraft, the public executioner, had arrived at Swansea
train station on the night before the planned execution. A large
crowd had gathered to see him and he emerged from the station a
rather corpulent figure, aged about fifty-five to sixty years of age.
He was immediately ushered into a carriage and transported to
the jail, where he then spent the night. The following morning
he was dressed in seedy black, with a gold chain displayed across

William Calcraft, Public Executioner. He hanged around 450 people including over thirty women in a forty-five year career. Paul Townsend

his chest. He had a reputation for effectively strangling his 'customers' rather than breaking their necks due to his continued use of a short drop. The crowd of onlookers at Swansea would have the dubious pleasure of seeing both methods unwittingly employed by Calcraft on the day.

Inside the jail a solemn stillness pervaded the atmosphere, far removed from the raucous scenes being enacted by the great congregation encamped outside its solid walls. The condemned men had retired between 8.00 and 9.00 pm the previous night before waking at midnight and then reading and conversing as they awaited their appointment with destiny. They had partaken of their last meal at 5.00 pm the night before and refused to take any sustenance on the morning itself.

At about 7.30 am their spiritual adviser, the Rev N Morpinos, took his leave of the duo, having spent some time in their presence on that fateful morning. At 7.40 am a mournful procession was formed close to the condemned cell. It consisted of the prison chaplain, the Rev E B Squire, the High Sheriff, the Deputy Sheriff, the Rev S Davies, the Rev E G Williams, Mr Hall (prison surgeon), Mr Wood (governor of Cardiff Prison) and several local prison officials. The Rev Morpinos was also present. On entering the cell it was noted the prisoners' demeanour was calm with no signs of bravado. William Calcraft, the public executioner, then pinioned the men's arms behind their backs while their necks were bared. No resistance of any description was offered by the condemned men. After exchanging a few words with their spiritual adviser the procession set off, having a distance of about 250 to 300 yards to cover before the scaffold was reached.

The chaplain led the way reading from the burial service as he went, with a condemned man on either side of him, their eyes downcast and their countenances sorrowful. On arrival on the scaffold the men fell to their knees and received a final few words from their priest, whose hand they kissed. They were now finally visible to a gathered crowd of about 18,000 people, whose upturned faces must have appeared as a sea before them. A subdued murmur ran through the crowd though there were no cries or insults from that quarter. Both men, clearly resigned to their fates, stepped firmly forward and placed themselves under the beam. Calcraft placed a white cap over the head of Selapatane, at the same time strapping his legs. While this was going on Alepis looked at the crowd with no visible sign of emotion. The same procedure was then followed for him.

Despite their arms being pinioned the condemned men managed to exchange a handshake and a few words with each other. They also contrived to shake the hand of the executioner. As a nearby clock tolled the eighth hour Calcraft slid the bolt and both men plummeted through the trap door. Alepis seemed to die almost instantly and without any sign of struggle. For Selapatane, however, it was not so easy and he was seen to struggle violently for around seven minutes though, happily, Calcraft was not required, as was sometimes the case in such events, to pull on the man's legs to speed his passing. As soon as the struggle had ended the crowd began to disperse. The bodies were left hanging for the customary one hour, as required by law, after which they were cut down and work commenced on dismantling the temporary scaffold. The bodies were duly buried within the precincts of the prison.

The *Cambrian* hoped that the unedifying spectacle would act as a fearful lesson that would not be forgotten by those in the town who might be contemplating evil. In an earlier edition it had bemoaned the fact that while the town's booming industries brought with them wealth, they also brought into the town ships' crews from all parts of the world, some of whose members then walked the town whilst being armed to the teeth. It was happy to report that the present case involved Greeks and not Welsh or Englishmen, and as Swansea had been free of murders for around a decade, it was comforting to note that the foreign ships, with half-civilised crews, rather than local men were the root cause of any problem of violence that might exist in the town.

CHAPTER 7

The Deadly Stowaways:
The *Hecla* and Yellow Fever
1865

*She was ... rolling about and
rambling ... her face was flushed
and dusky; skin very hot, and ...
very yellow ...*

On 26 July 1865 the barque *Hecla* set sail from Santiago, Cuba. Its destination was the port of Swansea in South Wales, where it would unload its cargo of copper ore at the wharf of the Cobre Copper Company. This raw material would then be processed at one of the numerous copper works in Swansea, a town which at the time dominated world copper processing, earning itself the nickname of 'Copperopolis'.

Aboard the wooden hulled *Hecla* were William Clouston, master, seventeen crew members and two passengers. Also aboard, largely unseen and unheard, were a number of passengers who did not appear on any ships' list or roster. These were tropical mosquitoes – of the *aedes aegypti* type – which had 'stowed away' in the ship's un-enclosed water butts and similar cool, damp places. The colder weather of the more northerly seas would usually have put an end to them, but on this voyage the weather was unusually warm and they were able to continue feeding and breeding as the voyage progressed.

Swansea, the port of destination for the *Hecla*, was at the time in the grip of a very warm autumn. Though medical science was unaware of it in 1865, mosquitoes of the type aboard the *Hecla* were carriers of yellow fever, a potentially fatal disease that was transmitted by the bite of the mosquito as it fed. It often fed on human blood and could thus pass on the virus to humans who had the misfortune to provide it with a meal. The disease was prevalent in

South American monkeys and a mosquito could become infected by biting such a monkey. Further spread of the disease then took place when an infected jungle mosquito, for example, bit a human who returned to civilisation in an infected condition to be bitten by another mosquito which in turn became infective. And so the process continued.

The disease transmission theory then prevailing amongst the medical profession was that disease was probably associated with filth and foul air ('foul miasmas') and that for many diseases, once the symptoms had developed, onward transmission from person to person was the usual method of infecting others. The role of mosquitoes in the process was quite unknown.

By the 8 September 1865 the *Hecla* was positioned about fifteen miles to the north east of Lundy Island, in the Bristol Channel. At 5.00 pm the barque was boarded by George Morgan, a Swansea pilot, who would guide the *Hecla* on the final approach to the North Dock at Swansea. The captain requested that Morgan summon some assistance from shore to help bring the ship into port. He explained that he had lost three crew members to illness on the journey from Cuba, had two men recovering from 'fever' and had another sailor suffering from what he termed as 'dropsy'.

Seafaring towns like Swansea and its coastal neighbours had no shortage of experienced mariners and five men were promptly brought on board to assist the depleted crew. With the extra hands quickly proving their worth, the *Hecla* was able to anchor close to the Mumbles roadstead, near Swansea, at about 9.00 pm, where it remained whilst displaying a light throughout the night.

At about 6.00 am on the 9 September 1865 the Swansea steam tug arrived and the *Hecla* was towed into the port of Swansea and duly moored at the Cobre Wharf on the North Dock. This wharf was situated on a small island around which the River Tawe flowed into the open sea. Despite losing crew members during the voyage and having men on board still seriously ill or recovering, the pre-caution of the ship lying outside the port and displaying a quarantine flag was not taken by Clouston, though the ship's flag was flown at half mast, leading to speculation in the town that crew members had been lost on the voyage. As relatives and friends of the local crew members thronged around the anchored vessel, anxious for news of loved ones, the scene became most distressing as bad news was imparted about the deaths of three crew members and the illness of several others.

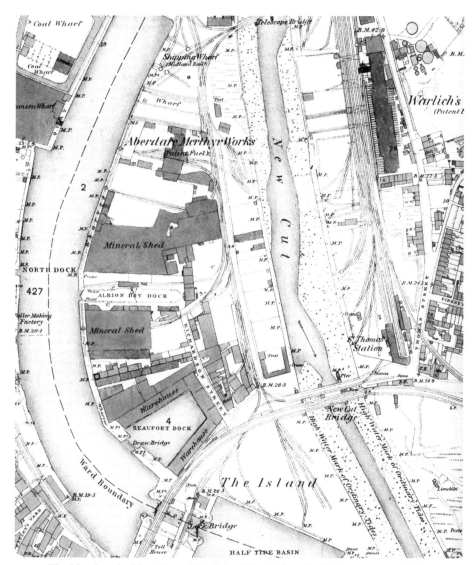

The Island on the River Tawe. The Cobre Wharf where the Hecla *was moored is the 'Mineral Shed' below the Albion Dry Dock.* West Glamorgan Archive Service

Subsequently, no report was made by Clouston to the port authorities about the crew losses sustained during the journey or the one crew member who was still unwell. This was a breach of the quarantine regulations then in force. Within an hour of arrival the sick man, together with the remaining ship's crew (including the two 'recovering' sailors), and two passengers went ashore and dispersed into the town. The *Hecla's* cargo hold hatches were then removed and gangs of men boarded the ship and began unloading the cargo of copper ore.

In a compact town like Swansea, news – especially bad news – travelled fast and by noon the Mayor had heard from his Sanitary Inspector that the recent arrival at the port had lost crew members on the voyage due to sickness. It had also offloaded a crew member who was adjudged to be seriously ill. The deaths were rumoured to have been caused by yellow fever and – by way of reasonable confirmation – the sick man, James Saunders, had been promptly seen by two local doctors who had diagnosed not dropsy, but the rather more deadly tropical disease of yellow fever. The post of mayor had a dual role at this time. In addition to his Swansea Corporation role as the pre-eminent citizen of the town, the mayor was also chairman of the local board of health, a creature created in Swansea in 1850 after the passing of the Public Health Act of 1848. The Swansea Board of Health was essentially the corporation in a different guise.

With commendable haste (and not a little bravery) the mayor, J Clarke Richardson, went to the captain of the *Hecla* and had the yellow fever rumours confirmed. There had indeed been deaths on the voyage that could be attributed to yellow fever and the sick man, Saunders, was believed by the captain to be suffering from the same affliction. In the company of Doctor Paddon the mayor next visited the house at Welcome Court where Saunders was lying, seriously ill. The house was found to be small and dirty and the room wretched.

Saunders was lying in bed and was so obviously close to death that no detailed medical examination was possible. However, it seemed that the illness was definitely not dropsy, as first claimed by Clouston, and it was observed that Saunders' body was tinged yellow, a clear indication of the likely presence of yellow fever. Within minutes of them leaving the house they were pursued by a crowd of local people to be given the news that Saunders was dead.

Grasping the possible seriousness of the situation, Doctor Paddon suggested some precautions which should be put into immediate effect. To this end the body of Saunders was placed inside a tarred sheet and he was hastily buried – within four hours of his death – at the recently opened Danygraig Cemetery. The house was then disinfected with lime-wash and chloride of lime, and nearby properties were treated in a similar manner. The bedding and clothing used by Saunders were also destroyed. As a final step, the mayor instructed the police to locate the crew and passengers of the *Hecla* and to ensure that their bodies, clothes and rooms were disinfected with chlorine. The *Hecla* was also disinfected though it remained moored at the Cobre Wharf.

Based on the medical knowledge of the time Paddon probably thought that he was taking sensible precautions to try and halt the further spread of the yellow fever outbreak. However, his measures – while of a cosmetic value as regards cleanliness – were hopelessly inadequate and, indeed, quite futile. When the *Hecla's* hatches had been opened the disturbed mosquitoes would have flown out from the shade and comfort of the hold. Finding the unusually warm Swansea weather much to their liking, they would have sought out some shady nooks and crannies, to await the cooler shade of dusk. When that arrived they would have gone in search of food. While the normal flight length of such a mosquito is less than 100 metres, sorties of up to 300 metres are by no means uncommon. This brought within their potentially deadly purview a respectable number of human targets, in what was a busy docks area, with some nearby – and frequently squalid – housing.

Typically, mosquitoes of this type would bite every four days on average. Where temperatures dropped below about sixty degrees fahrenheit, the flight and bite activities were greatly reduced and breeding ceased. In Swansea in 1865 only five days in the first fifteen days of September showed a minimum temperature below sixty degrees, allowing plenty of scope for mosquito activity. Once a victim was bitten it was likely that the onset of symptoms would become evident between four and seven days after infection. Dr Paddon, of course, was blissfully unaware of these facts, or their role in disease transmission. He had done what seemed prudent and now had to simply await events.

With what seemed to be sensible precautions in place and with the most serious case having been rapidly despatched to a common grave in the local cemetery, there would have been no major cause for concern amongst the population of Swansea. Indeed, the meteorological registrar, Mr Rosser, would later confirm that, over the years, several sufferers of yellow fever had been brought ashore at Swansea to convalesce or die. What was unknown in the port of Swansea (or indeed any port in the whole of Britain then or since) was for the disease to somehow spread from a ship-borne victim to the local populace. There was no reason to suppose that this pattern would change in the present circumstances.

Such comforting suppositions proved, however, to be sadly misplaced on this occasion. A ship's rigger named Norman had boarded the *Hecla* on the day of its arrival, 9 September 1865. He had boarded to visit the chief mate and had been on board when the ailing Saunders had been lowered ashore over the side of the vessel. He was only on board for about a quarter of an hour. On the morning of 15 September he had awoken 'feeling dull' and with pain in the head and lower parts of the stomach. He also felt bilious, though he did not vomit. By the 17 September his condition had worsened and he had an intense headache, a noisy delirium and slight yellowness of the skin. This was accompanied by 'urgent vomiting'. He remained in this state for four days but then began to slowly improve. By 1 October he was reported as '... sweating freely ... pulse weak, has been as low as 48; tongue quite clean, rather red; appetite returning; urine reported to be "very brown", plentiful; much jaundiced ... two abscesses ...' However, he was over the worst of it and recovered in due course.

David Bowen, aged thirty-three years, was a Customs House officer, and he had been deputed to patrol the quay alongside the moored *Hecla* from the 10 September onwards. This he did diligently until, on 17 September, he was taken ill with sudden headaches and back pain. On 19 September he was seen by Dr Griffiths '... in bed; face and eyes much infected; skin intensely hot and dry; no jaundice; tongue moist, with much white fur; complete anorexia; no vomiting, but some nausea; pulse 110–120. Pain in head and back, with fever ...' After this visit Dr Griffiths himself became ill, though it is doubtful whether this was due to yellow fever.

When seen by Dr Wilks on 21 September, Bowen '... was vomiting after all food, and after every dose of a hydrocyanic acid mixture. Vomit looked like coffee grounds, and was offensive, with an almost faecal odour ...' By 4.00 pm it had proved necessary to cease administering medicine and food and only ice was proffered to the by now seriously ill Bowen. At 7.00 pm vomiting was copious and frequent and was black in colour and shortly afterwards medicines – including ether and chloroform – were again administered as an emergency measure. On the morning of 22 September, somewhat surprisingly, Bowen was able to declare that he felt much better and would be able to go out with his wife, had he not been so weak. However, by 2.00 pm he was delirious, in a state of collapse, cold, and his complexion was blue. He died later in the evening, the first land-based fatality attributable to the *Hecla*'s deadly stowaways.

On the 18 September 1865, the day after Bowen had first fallen ill, Margaret Brown, aged twenty, who lived with her husband at her father's family's home, about 160 yards from the Cobre Wharf, began to exhibit signs of illness. In the week preceding her illness she had frequently visited her father, who was in charge of a ship moored near the *Hecla*. Starting with sudden pains in the loins and head, by the following day she was prostrate in bed when seen by Mr Shepherd. She was feverish with a quick pulse and a dry, brown tongue. Food and water was vomited back. The pain was so intense that for a time smallpox was suspected and it later proved necessary to relieve her bowels by means of medicine and an injection. By the third day after the onset she '. . . began to vomit black stuff; looking like thin soot and water, and became delirious. On Thursday 21st found much worse . . .' During the afternoon her:

> *. . . delirium ceased. Her skin was cooler, her tongue still dry, her strength was less, but she was not actually collapsed, and in the evening the vomiting ceased. She felt more comfortable, and looked better. Soon after 8 o'clock a.m. on September 22nd, Mr. Shepherd was fetched to her, and found her dead.*

As was seen in the case of Bowen an apparent improvement in health had proven to be short lived, with a sudden relapse resulting in a speedy death and the dashed hopes of family and friends for a patient's full recovery.

John Jesse was twenty-four years old and was an apprentice in Richardson's shipbuilding yard. There he was engaged in daily work at the 'patent slip' of the yard and this was adjacent to the Cobre Wharf, where the *Hecla* was discharging her cargo. He was taken ill on 20 September and was seen by Mr Davies's assistant. He was found to have '. . . a hot skin, flushed face, delirium; with tongue red, dry in the centre . . . vomiting all his food . . . pulse full, over 100 . . .'

On 22 September he rallied and had a slower pulse and a cleaner tongue. As in other cases this improvement was not maintained; on 22 September he was seen to be vomiting constantly and was strongly jaundiced. He did not complain of much pain at this time

Burial register entry for Margaret Brown. The grave is clearly a 'common' one with unrelated people being buried in it until it was full. The author, by permission of the Registrar of cemeteries, Swansea City Council

Burial register entry for John Jesse. Another 'common' grave, this one contains mainly infant bodies. The author, by permission of the Registrar of cemeteries, Swansea City Council

but he was in a collapsed and half comatose state. He could not be roused and died later in the evening, in the midst of a further attack of vomiting.

On the day of the first three land-based fatalities – 22 September 1865 – the weekly edition of the *Cambrian* was published. It is clear from its editorial that the town was largely unaware of the suffering and deaths that had befallen several of its citizens following the arrival of the *Hecla*. The *Cambrian* was only concerned with the fate of the crew and noted that it did '... not pretend to decide whether or not it was Yellow Fever, from which those unfortunate seamen died ...' It went on to criticise those (it did not specify whom) that had failed to prevent the entry of the vessel into port. Perversely, it then sympathized with the master and crew in the scenario of a ship wracked by fever, with all hands supposedly constrained to stay on board under the usual quarantine laws, when the comforts of land were so close. It posed the question:

> ... *would there be much danger to the multitude in removing these men from their infected prison? We should not think that in ordinary circumstances there would be more, if a proper place of reception were provided for patients, than is connected with a fever hospital. At any rate we find that in the case referred to no evil effects followed, and there is not the slightest occasion for alarm with regard to it ...*

In its 15 September issue it had mused on the desirability of the town having a suitable hospital for the reception of returning sailors who had brought back disease from foreign waters. It noted that there was considerable local apprehension on the dangers of contagious disease being introduced into the town. However, no such secure facility existed in Swansea so there was little alternative other than to bring the sick ashore from such ships.

In the 22 September issue, in a letter to the newspaper, Doctor Paddon pondered over the supposed link between filth and contagious disease. He was not entirely convinced of a direct link, suggesting that the filth needed a 'seed' to trigger an outbreak of the more familiar British perils of gastric fever, cholera or typhus. In the case of yellow fever he accepted that only in exceptional circumstances could such a tropical disease propagate itself in Britain as usually the more northerly climatic conditions worked against its spread. However, Paddon wondered whether a visitation of ship-borne yellow fever acted as the 'seed' for a subsequent outbreak of severe gastric fever on land? He felt it did so based on previous instances, and for that reason it was important to uphold the quarantine regulations. Paddon had written this letter on 21 September 1865, a day before the three land-based deaths took place.

On the same day that Margaret Brown and John Jesse had fallen ill – 18 September – Margaret Williams, a servant at a house that abutted onto the Cobre Wharf, also became ill. The early symptoms must have been becoming familiar to some of the medical men of Swansea, by this time. Vomiting, pain in the head, back, loins and legs were all present. By the 23rd she was '... rolling about and rambling, complaining of no localized pain, but pain all over. Her face was flushed and dusky; skin very hot, and conjunctive very yellow. Vomiting frequently ...'

Calomel and colocynth were administered and by 29 September the symptoms began to abate. Happily, on this occasion, this was not to be the deadly herald of a sudden relapse and death. By 1 October the vomiting had ceased and by the 3rd she had sat up and been able to eat food on three consecutive days. Though suffering from moderate weight loss and giddy spells a good recovery was subsequently made.

If the *Cambrian* newspaper had found no undue cause for concern in its issue of 22 September (when probably only the death of Saunders was definitely linked by the newspaper to the *Hecla* and yellow fever) by the 29 September edition things had moved on apace. By that time, in addition to Saunders, no less than eleven citizens of Swansea had fatally succumbed to what was now accepted to be 'true' yellow fever. Four more would die after 29 September. Another six people were suffering or would suffer under its effects, though they would eventually recover. A number of other cases were suspected, but unconfirmed, as being caused by yellow fever.

The *Cambrian* referred to the '... very exaggerated reports ...' that were currently circulating in the town and sought to allay public fears. It also mentioned the arrival of Doctor Buchanan, of the London Fever Hospital, who had been sent to Swansea by a concerned government in order to investigate the situation. The newspaper hoped that the *Hecla* would soon be removed outside the port, an option that the mayor had found himself legally powerless to order, in the face of opposition from the vessel owners (who were keen to see a valuable cargo offloaded). There were also rumours in the town that the mayor was commercially linked to the *Hecla*'s owners and had therefore been unduly lenient in his

George Buchanan of the London Fever Hospital. After investigating yellow fever in Swansea he became the government's Chief Medical Officer in 1879, holding that post until 1892. Department of Health

dealings over it. This he most vehemently denied and it did seem that there was no truth in the allegation.

Unaware of the role played by the mosquitoes in the transmission of the disease it was natural that the evidence that was gathered relating to the deaths tended to show that all the afflicted had been in contact with the *Hecla*, or had been in its vicinity, for some reason. In reality, the relatively short flight span of the mosquito (300 metres at most) limited the risk to those who, for whatever reason, came into fairly close proximity to the *Hecla* or the North Dock. For example, Sarah Wilson lived and worked at Richardson's shipyard. Falling ill on 22 September 1865, she was dead by 25 September. William Thomas was another who worked at the shipyard and he duly died on 29 September after apparently having encountered a mosquito from the *Hecla*.

John Colwell worked as a smithy near to the shipyards of the Island. He was dead by 24 September, while four employees of

Bath's Yard also fell ill, of which three subsequently died. The Mahoney family was particularly hard hit. Living at Cobre Row, and thus very close to the wharf where the *Hecla* lay, no less than five family members fell ill, with three of them being confirmed as yellow fever cases. Of these three, two later died while all other family members eventually recovered.

James Hickey was the landlord of the *Pelican Inn*. He was taken ill on 20 September and, along with the usual symptoms, developed an appearance of severe jaundice. However, he was well recovered by the 1 October, when he was seen by Mr Buchanan of the London Fever Hospital, in the course of his governmental investigation. Not so fortunate was Hickey's wife, Elizabeth, who fell ill on 22 September. On 25 September she miscarried a child of five months development, and then her own health gradually worsened until her death on the following day.

Two men who were aboard the sloop *Eleanor* at the North Dock fell ill, with one later dying at Llanelli while the other recovered. Two others who lived at Cobre Row also became infected with the first dying on the 1st and the other on 5 October. This latter case was the last death attributed to the outbreak.

An examination of the Parliamentary report and other papers related to the outbreak was completed by modern day medical experts in the 1980s. It concluded that a close study of the pattern of infection and the life cycle of the mosquito indicated that at least fifty-seven infected mosquitoes had been released from the *Hecla*. These could have bred on land in the then prevailing weather conditions, but by the time their offspring had matured enough to become infective (around five weeks) the outbreak had effectively passed. The newly born mosquitoes would have found no already infected victims to pick up the disease from and so they played no part in furthering the outbreak. It was the coming of colder weather that caused the original batch of infected mosquitoes to cease biting and later die, and the epidemic then to fizzle out.

The outbreak had repercussions far beyond the confines of Swansea. It featured on several occasions in *The Times* where the tone was generally low key and supportive, though the non-removal of the *Hecla* from port at an early stage was deplored. Though ignorant of the means of transmission of the disease *The Times* was able to deduce that in the Swansea incident, and several others from the continent to which it referred, it seemed to be the unusually warm autumn weather that was the exacerbating factor.

An aedes aegypti *type mosquito biting a human. Its role in the transmission of disease was unknown until 1898.* (Wiki Media [public domain])

Given that this was not typical of the British climate it hoped that the normal seasonal change would prevent a reoccurrence, except under the most unusual circumstances.

There can be no doubt that the trade of the town was affected both during and after the outbreak. In a letter to *The Times* dated 14 October 1865, Mr J Williams James, General Superintendent of Swansea Harbour, pleaded for the insertion in the newspaper of a resolution recently made by members of the medical profession in Swansea. This declaration gave Swansea a clean bill of health. He explained that vessels leaving the port of Swansea were being subjected to rigorous quarantine requirements on arrival at ports in France, Italy and Spain and this was interfering with normal trade arrangements and would also have been adding to crew costs as voyage times were lengthened. However, no new yellow fever cases had been reported in Swansea for almost two weeks and that fact, coupled with the falling temperatures, meant that the Swansea medical men were united in their belief that the disease had run its course. Therefore, normal shipping movements from Swansea should be resumed without unnecessary restriction by foreign authorities.

So difficult did the issue become that by the end of October 1865 a deputation of Swansea ship owners and merchants, together with the port superintendent, visited the Foreign Office at London to personally present a memorial. This asked the Foreign Secretary to make representations on the matter via the British Ambassador to Spain, a country which was proving particularly unyielding over the issue of quarantine requirements. Naturally, with the passing of time and the growing evidence of no further infections at Swansea, trade did eventually get back to normal.

The outbreak at Swansea in 1865 is the only occasion when mosquitoes infected with yellow fever got ashore in Britain and transmitted the disease to local people. Despite the great concern caused by the incident at the time, Swansea got off relatively lightly, with only fifteen deaths amongst a population of over 40,000. Every death was a tragedy, of course, for the family and friends of those afflicted, but had the *Hecla* arrived at the height of the hot weather it is entirely possible that breeding and then flight and bite activities would have taken place over a longer period, with a correspondingly higher death rate.

The medical knowledge of the time provided absolutely no protection, of course, being unaware of the means of transmission and having no effective cure. One benefit was that the fatalities attributed to the outbreak and its effect on trade galvanised the local health board to appoint a medical officer of health, a move that was endorsed with acclaim by the *Cambrian* newspaper. This post had been filled some years earlier but had then complacently been allowed to lapse following the resignation of the then incumbent.

Further improvements followed as a result of the Sanitary Act of 1866, which placed the inspection of ships under the local board of health of the port in question, a matter which had previously been under the remit of the Poor Law Guardians due to their role in vaccinations. So, by way of consolation, at least some good eventually came out of the bad that had befallen the town of Swansea. Nevertheless, it would be over a quarter century in the future before experiments conducted by the American Army based in Cuba, during the Spanish-American War of 1898, revealed the role of the mosquito in the transmission of yellow fever.

CHAPTER 8

An Intemperate Woman: The Death of Mrs Lake
1868

What is that state your wife is in?

At about 11.15 pm on Saturday, 7 March 1868, Stephen Hicks of Earl Street, Hafod, Swansea, was in the act of getting ready for bed when his attention was drawn to a loud knocking on the door of his house. Outside his front door was William Lake, a neighbour, who asked that Hicks come at once to Lake's house. His wife, Lake said, was 'dead or dying'.

As they hurried towards the house Lake explained that he had found his wife in a shallow drainage pit in the garden of the house. He had managed to get her into the house but was apparently so concerned at her condition that he had sought the urgent assistance of Hicks. On entering the house and going to the kitchen Hicks was shocked to see Mrs Lake sitting in an armchair, her head resting against the wall. There were cuts over her right eye, and marks on her left breast and hand. On touching her hand and finding it quite cold, Hicks concluded that Mrs Lake was dead.

Dismissing Lake's suggestion that they try and get her into bed, Hicks sent him instead for a doctor. Mrs Harvey, another neighbour, had arrived by this time, as well as Hicks's wife who promptly fainted as she took in the awful scene. Doctor Lewis arrived quickly and observed that the woman had been killed, implying that this was not an accidental death. Lake made no comment on this remark or its implications. With Lewis unable to offer any medical assistance he instead busied himself by going in search of a police constable.

As Hicks waited he noticed a three legged stool that appeared to have blood on its flat surface and he also observed that there was blood on the left leg of Lake's trousers. The floor of the room was wet, as if a half hearted attempt had been made to wash it. At this

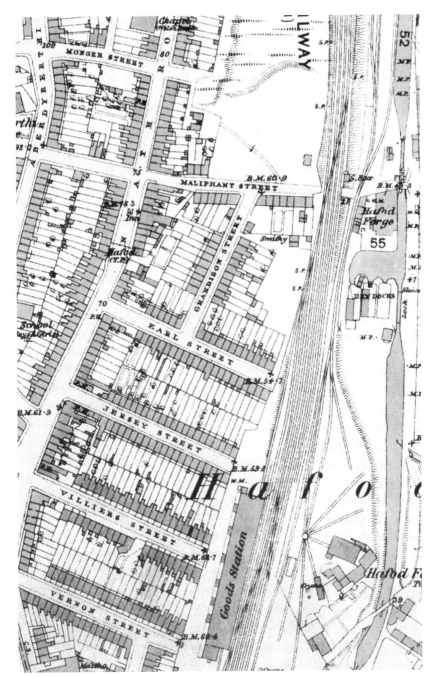

Map showing the location of Earl Street, Swansea. West Glamorgan Archive Service

point Police Constable Francis Jones arrived, having been summoned by Doctor Lewis. Quickly assessing the scene that confronted him, he asked Lake 'What is that state your wife is in?' Lake replied that she had been drunk all week and as regards the cuts on her face it was 'No odds to you – I will do something to myself before night'.

The guarding of the house was entrusted to Police Constable Thomas who happened to live in the same street and had now arrived on the scene. At the same time Police Constable Jones placed Lake under arrest and escorted him to the police station, foiling an attempt by Lake to run away during the process. On being charged with the murder of his wife, Lake simply stated that he was innocent.

Before leaving the house Hicks went upstairs to bring away Lake's young son, who was still sleeping soundly in bed, so that he could spend the remainder of the night in a safe place. On gathering the child from bed Hicks noticed what seemed to be blood in the room though, still unnerved by what he had witnessed downstairs, he did not linger to make a more detailed examination.

These facts were recounted at the inquest into Mrs Lake's death. It was when Doctor Paddon described the results of his post mortem examination that the full horror of what had happened at the house that night became all too apparent. Describing Mrs Lake as a 'small, but rather spare, well formed, and under-nourished person' he went on to note that there were two clean cut wounds to the forehead area, both of which had cut through to the bone. There was bruising to the forehead and scalp, the chin, an area above the left collar bone and both arms and elbows.

Much worse was to follow; four of the ribs on the right side were found to be sharply broken off and the liver resting behind these ribs was described as 'pulped'. It was the injury to the liver, Doctor Paddon concluded, that had caused death. He did not believe that such fractures of the ribs could be sustained in an accident. It was, he opined, quite likely that such injuries had been caused by a powerful kick from the toe of an iron tipped boot. Paddon also believed that the injuries to the head were not the result of, say, a single fall as they were present in several places. Additionally, the cuts could not have been self-inflicted.

The evidence having been heard, the Coroner summed up what he said was a very serious case and took time to distinguish between what might constitute murder as opposed to manslaughter.

The gate at Swansea Prison in 2009, little changed since William Lake was held there pending his trial. The author

After a retirement of one hour and twenty-five minutes the jury returned to declare a verdict of 'wilful murder'. William Lake would now have to account for his alleged actions at the summer assizes.

The case opened on 24 July 1868, with Mr Bowen and Mr W H Michael prosecuting, while Mr Giffard, QC, was counsel for Lake, under a special warrant from the Queen. The prisoner pleaded 'not guilty' in a decisive voice and proceeded to take the greatest interest in the evidence presented. As the facts were unfolded issues that might have appeared to the casual observer to represent a clear cut case, soon became not quite so distinct.

With the prosecution having outlined the broad facts surrounding Mrs Lake's sad demise the first significant witness was John Lake, aged nineteen years, the son of the deceased. John Lake recounted how his mother had been a woman of intemperate habits. She was much prone to indulging heavily in drink, to the obvious frustration of her hard working husband (though he himself was not unduly averse to a tipple). Indeed John recalled his father begging on his bended knees that his wife should rein in her excessive drinking, but to no avail. He described a mother who drank away the house-keeping and left the house untended. Against the prevailing standards of the day she did no cleaning and prepared no food. She had also pawned household goods to supplement the money available to her for the purchase of alcohol.

His mother had, he said, been more or less constantly under the influence of alcohol for the entire three weeks preceding her death. A new suit purchased by her husband had found its way to the pawn shop, the proceeds being quickly squandered on drink. By contrast her husband was described as a largely industrious man, who was very good towards his wife, though John had to admit that his father had been bound over to keep the peace following a scuffle with the deceased sometime earlier. John Lake sobbed repeatedly during the course of his evidence.

Margaret Casey was sworn in and stated that she had seen Mrs Lake in the *Ancient Briton* public house at about 9.00 pm on the night in question. Mrs Lake had been seen to consume both beer and gin before being helped out of the inn, clearly the worse for drink, by Mrs Sparks. With Mrs Lake unwilling or unable to say where she lived, some young girls had directed the couple to her home in Earl Street, where Mrs Sparks wished her a good night and watched her safely enter the house. Other neighbours confirmed that Mrs Lake seemed inebriated and one recalled hearing some noise from the Lake household at between 9.00 and 10.00 pm. It had sounded as if someone was raking out the grate, but it seemed of no particular importance at the time. It was at 10.00 pm that Stephen Hicks had been called by William Lake and told that Lake's wife was dead or dying and he now testified to that effect at the trial.

The trial jury then heard the disturbing medical evidence of Doctor Paddon. He explained that he did not believe that the rib injuries could have been caused by a fall. Indeed, he was sure that they were the result of a kick and agreed that the boots of the defendant – as produced by Inspector Brooks – matched his deductions as to what might have caused the injuries. Additionally, he placed the several face wounds as having occurred an hour before death, indicating that Mrs Lake had been subject to more than one instance of assault. Interestingly, he added that he had known the defendant for a long time and knew him to be industrious, hard working and steady.

With the prosecution case now complete Mr Giffard rose from his seat to deliver a speech in favour of William Lake that he hoped would spare him from a meeting with the public executioner. He reminded the jury that it now bore a heavy responsibility and that it must be satisfied of guilt beyond a reasonable doubt, were it to convict.

Giffard remarked on the absence of a motive. He described a man constantly struggling to keep his family respectable despite his wife's repeated drunkenness. He had even gone down on his bended knees in a forlorn attempt to turn his wife away from her self-destructive path but had been answered only with oaths and curses.

He argued that in the peculiar circumstances of this case it was entirely likely that the injuries had been inflicted without pre-meditation and were the result of a sudden and uncontrollable impulse. The prosecution had no evidence that Lake had been in the house at the time the injuries were inflicted. There had been no evidence of an argument or row; indeed the only sound that had been heard had been the stirring of ashes in the grate.

The blood on the prisoner was consistent with his, as he had claimed, having found his wife injured outside the house and carrying her in. As to Doctor Paddon's views on how the injuries had been caused, Giffard claimed that the doctor was an expert on injuries and whether they had caused death, but no more. As regards how the injuries had been caused then the jury were quite as expert as the esteemed doctor. Mrs Lake was extremely drunk on the night; who was to say that she had not fallen and injured herself?

Even if it was accepted that William Lake had in fact attacked his wife who could doubt that it was an impulsive and unpremeditated outburst, resulting from his wife's intemperate habits? That being the case then the prosecution charge should be immediately re-duced to that of manslaughter.

The judge then summed up explaining that the first question was whether Lake had inflicted the terrible injuries that had resulted in the death of his wife. The second question was whether the circumstances were such that the charge of murder made against Lake should be reduced to one of manslaughter. The other possibilities of death by accident or by the hand of a person or persons unknown were also alluded to.

The jury then retired and after a deliberation of thirty minutes returned to record a verdict of manslaughter. The judge noted that in his opinion the jury had taken a very lenient view of the case. Despite the repeated provocations proffered by Mrs Lake there was no excuse for the savagery which had ended in her death. The case was a very bad one and one that – despite the finding of the jury – verged on one of murder. Sentence was then passed that Lake be held in penal servitude for a period of twelve years.

It seems that the catalogue of bad behaviour that Lake's wife had subjected him to had counted in his favour. Mrs Lake's own son had provided powerful evidence in that respect. Whilst the jury did not go so far as to say that he was entirely innocent, due allowance had been made for a man who may simply have been tipped over the edge by his wife's repeatedly intolerable behaviour.

CHAPTER 9

The Jealous Husband:
The Killing of Mrs Duncan
1872

She knew my temper well ...

Police Constable John Lewis commenced his shift of duty at 6.00 am on 25 October 1872, and proceeded to patrol the area of Swansea's Welcome Lane, wondering what the day would bring his way. He did not have to wait long before his curiosity was satisfied. Only five minutes later he was approached by a man – dripping wet though it was not raining – who said simply 'Here, I give myself to your hands'. Somewhat startled Police Constable Lewis asked the man as to what it was he had done. With a chilling directness the man responded 'I have murdered my wife and have been at the dock to drown myself. I jumped into the water, but I thought I would not drown myself or run'.

In response to further questions the man indicated that he had killed his wife with a flat iron, and she now lay in their house on the Strand, near the foundry, a distance of about 150 yards. They duly entered the house and ascended the stairs, pausing for the man to change his wet clothes, before entering the middle room of three on the first floor. There were three small children in bed in the room, as well as a babe in arms. On the bed lay Emma Duncan, the wife of Andrew Joseph Duncan. Cradled in her arm was the baby. It was Mr Duncan who had brought Police Constable Lewis to the house. Mrs Duncan was bleeding heavily from the head, the blood soaking both the pillow and the floor. She was alive but unconscious.

Summoned by a shrill blast on a police whistle, Police Constable Henry Smith arrived at the scene. Duncan told him 'I have killed my wife. There is a hole through the wall and a man there is looking at my wife. I have cautioned her about it several times before. She always denied it, but I now saw him myself, and she knew my temper well.'

The Strand, Swansea, under water. Its proximity to the docks made it attractive to sailors but high tides or heavy rain could cause flooding as shown here. West Glamorgan Archive Service

The policemen removed Duncan to the police station and summoned medical assistance for Mrs Duncan. Mr D H Thomas was a member of the Royal College of Surgeons, and he attended at the house in the company of Police Constable Smith. He found Mrs Duncan still insensible on the bed, her baby remaining cradled in her arms and sleeping soundly. On removing her nightcap he found six wounds, of which four were lacerations and two incisions. Brain tissue protruded through three of the lacerations. Such was the ferocity of the attack that the skull had clearly been fractured. There was a bloodstained flat iron in the room and it was reasonable to conclude that this was the assault weapon as far as the lacerations were concerned. The incisions would have been caused by a sharp instrument and Mr Thomas duly observed a razor that had been found between the bed and the mattress. The room was examined by the police and, though there were gaps in the wallpaper, there was no sign whatsoever of a 'hole' through which someone could have peered from an adjoining room.

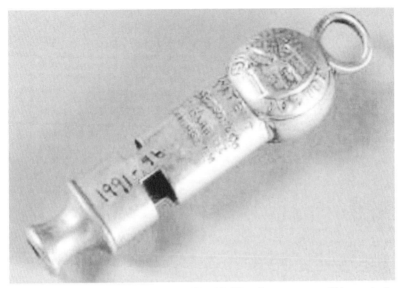

A police whistle. Surprisingly, whistles like this Victorian one were still in use in the 1970s, before the advent of personal radios. South Wales Police Museum

Mr Thomas returned to the police station at 8.00 am and observed the prisoner, though he did not carry out an examination. Duncan was visibly excited and trembling although in other respects he seemed in control of himself. Thomas suspected that the man was possibly a heavy drinker, and the shaking was a manifestation of *delirium tremens*. In the meantime further enquiries were underway on the Strand.

Martha Jones was the wife of Mr Jones the tailor, and lived in the *Crown* public house on the Strand, which was next door to the house of the prisoner. Mrs Jones recalled that at about 4.00 am on the night in question she had been awoken by a woman's voice repeatedly calling 'Murder!' accompanied by the sound of children screaming. Jones's husband did not bestir himself from his bed and Mrs Jones contented herself with only peering nervously into the street from a window. The Strand, being close to the port and popular with mariners, was at that time a street with a reputation for rowdy behavior and such commotions would not have been unusual. The cries continued until after 5.00 am though by that time they seemed to be getting feebler.

The evidence of Mrs Jones contradicted the medical opinion of Mr Thomas, since Thomas felt that the head wounds inflicted at

A police rattle, used to summon assistance and occasionally brandished as a make-shift weapon. They were replaced by whistles in the 1880s. South Wales Police Museum

about 4.00 am would have rendered the victim unconscious and thus unable to repeatedly call out as late as 5.00 am.

Passing the house of the prisoner at about 6.05 am had been John Griffiths, a blacksmith who had a foundry on the Strand. He was alerted by the cries of the children and his attention was also attracted by Mrs Jones, who stated that cries of 'murder' had been heard from the house. At this juncture Griffiths saw the prisoner leaving the house dressed in a shirt, drawers and stockings only to return soon afterwards in the company of a policeman.

Given the severity of Mrs Duncan's wounds it proved impossible to remove her to the hospital. Whilst treatment was administered in the house it proved ineffective and, after lingering for about twelve hours after the presumed time of the attack, she duly breathed her last.

These then were the facts that were placed before a jury by Mr Hughes, prosecuting, at the trial of Andrew Joseph Duncan, which took place in March 1873. The charge was that he had feloniously, wickedly and with malice aforethought murdered his wife. The prisoner at the bar appeared unconcerned at his dire position and merely gazed around the room, smiling repeatedly.

The jury having heard the case for the prosecution it became apparent that the defence, led by Mr B T Williams, intended to call no witnesses whatsoever. In summing up for the prosecution Hughes thought he saw clearly the path down which the defence hoped to lead the jury. He anticipated a defence claim of insanity on the ground that there appeared to be no motive for the crime and a man who therefore committed such an atrocious act, without any apparent reason must, by simple logic, be deemed insane. Hughes pointed out to the jury that the defence had had every opportunity to present such a defence but had not done so. No evidence had been produced to support a claim of insanity and he hoped that the jury would carefully consider instead all the evidence that had, in fact, been produced by the prosecution that supported a charge of murder.

The defence summing up did indeed proceed down the path that Hughes had alluded to. Mr Williams painted a picture of a loving family man who had suddenly fallen upon his wife in a shocking attack, perpetrated in the presence of his own children. Were these the actions of a sane man, he asked? What sane man would tell a policeman that a man was looking at his wife through a hole in the wall when, it was obvious from the most cursory inspection, that no such hole existed in the wall? It was the con-clusion of the defence team that Duncan had been in a state of mind which rendered him not responsible for his actions on that fateful morning. The fact of his having immersed himself in the sobering cold water of the harbour might have played some part in his later appearing quite calm when seen by the medical men.

The Judge explained to the jury that they were fortunate in that, unlike in certain other difficult cases, they had no doubt as to the identity of the person who had inflicted the mortal wounds on Mrs Duncan. There was nothing in the evidence that suggested that a finding of manslaughter would better suit the circumstances of the case before them. They need simply find the accused guilty of murder or, if that was not their belief, then the other option was that he was 'not guilty on account of the state of mind in which he was in when he committed the crime'. Indeed, in this particular case the state of mind of the prisoner at the bar was the only question that required their earnest consideration. The law was quite clear: every man was considered sane and thus responsible for his acts until it was proved to the contrary. If it had been proved that at the time of the offence Duncan, because of the state of his mind, did not know right from wrong, then he must have been insane.

The jury then retired and, after a lapse of a little less than thirty minutes, re-entered the room. On the question being put, the jury foreman, Mr Evan Crapper, responded with a single word – 'guilty'. The Judge then donned the black cap and in a hushed court pronounced sentence in the usual form, adding that he concurred with the verdict, being unable to see any evidence that Duncan did not know what he was doing on that fateful morning. He held out no hope of a possible commutation of the sentence of death and suggested that a pardon was now only possible from a divine, rather than a worldly, power. Duncan heard the sentence with no visible show of emotion.

It is interesting to note that at this time medical opinion was not obtained at an early stage for presentation at the trial. Of course the medical profession was only then gaining some credibility as knowledge advanced and diligent intervention became based more on practical experience and the results of experiment, rather than merely well informed hunches or guesswork. Whilst that was the case for those branches of the medical fraternity that dealt with physical problems, the same could not be said as regards psychiatry and its associated areas which were still in their infancy.

In Duncan's case, however, help proved to be at hand and it did not, in fact, require the divine intervention referred to by the judge. The *Cambrian* newspaper rather sniffily reported on 28 March 1873 that the Home Office had issued a statement which read:

> *The Secretary of State having since the conviction of Andrew Joseph Duncan, at the late Glamorgan Assizes, of murder, received memorials containing fresh facts bearing upon the case, which memorials were referred by him to the learned Judge who presided at the trial, and the Judge having recommended that there should be medical inquiry as to the state of the prisoner's mind, Mr. Bruce . . . directed Dr. Orange*

and Dr. Briscoe to make such inquiry; and they having reported their opinion that the prisoner was insane when he committed the murder, and still is so, Mr. Bruce has, with the concurrence of the learned Judge, advised her Majesty to respite the capital sentence.

Duncan was instead to be detained 'at Her Majesty's pleasure' in a criminal lunatic asylum.

The *Cambrian* reported that the result was not popular within the town though, it added with some satisfaction, at least the town had been spared the unsavoury ordeal of an execution, even if it were to take place in private, behind the high walls of the prison. The newspaper apparently echoed the view of the town-folk that the process by which Duncan had been spared a meeting with the hangman was defective. It stated:

After carefully weighing a large amount of evidence – tendered publicly by witnesses sworn to tell the truth, and subjected to the test of skillful cross-examination – a jury of twelve 'good men' found the prisoner guilty, rejecting as unproved the plea of his advocate that he was of unsound mind when he committed the crime, a plea in support of which scarcely a particle of evidence was offered.

It went on to disparage the finding of 'fresh facts', the detail of which was not known in the town, as was the reason why these facts were not advanced at the trial thus giving the prosecution an opportunity to rebut them. It added:

... the result is that upon the faith of statements and opinions of which the public know nothing, the verdict of the jury is set aside, the sentence of the Judge rescinded, and the prisoner in effect is declared to be 'not guilty' of wilful murder, but simply a sufferer from mental disease.

A telegram advising of the probability of a respite in sentence had been received by the prison governor on the Saturday afternoon, and this was confirmed by the arrival of a messenger at midnight the same day. The *Cambrian* concluded its story by saying that the changed situation 'was communicated to the prisoner, who received it with scarcely the slightest visible emotion. Indeed, if the most stolid indifference, an utter absence of any sign of sensibility, be a sign of insanity, there can be little reason to doubt that Duncan is insane'.

CHAPTER 10

Those in Peril on the Sea: The *Caswell* Mutiny
1876

Now boys, for your lives!

In 1875 Captain George William Best had good reason to be satisfied with his position in life. A skilled and experienced mariner, his social standing had been additionally enhanced by his marriage to the daughter of Mr Allison, the Chief Constable of Swansea. He had also recently been entrusted by Messrs W H Tucker & Co. of Swansea, with taking the barque *Caswell* on her first major voyage from Glasgow to Buenos Aires.

The Swansea registered *Caswell* had been built at Dumbarton in 1875 by Messrs McKellar, McMillen & Co. It was 156 feet long and 28 feet wide, with a gross weight of 499 tons. Fitted to the best modern standards, the *Caswell* had cost in the region of £10,000 to build. She had been designed with the stormy passages around the Cape Horn in mind, and as such could cope with very severe weather conditions. Sadly, in the subsequent relatively short working life of the *Caswell*, it would be found that the storms that blew up between her decks would be almost as deadly as any she encountered in the open sea.

Captain Best – a man of above average height, ruddy complexion and dark hair – set out with the *Caswell* from Glasgow on 1 July 1875 with a cargo of iron water pipes. The plan was to offload these at Buenos Aires and then seek out a cargo in or around that port that could be transported back to a British sea port. The currently pristine ship was to be very much a workhorse, transporting whatever cargoes came its way between the two continents so as to maximise the economic benefit for its Swansea based owners.

After seventy-three days the *Caswell* arrived at Buenos Aires and promptly offloaded her cargo. If at first sight all seemed well, such

Map of South America showing Antofogasta, Valparaiso and Buenos Aires, all destinations on the Caswell's *ill-fated voyage.* Tourizm Maps, 2003

an appearance was, in fact, deceptive. Though details are scant it is apparent that there had been friction between the captain and the crew during the voyage to South America. Indeed, two thirds of the outbound crew of nineteen – which consisted mainly of Scottish mariners – decided not to return to Britain in the *Caswell*. They chose instead to mope around a foreign port, far from home and loved ones, until they finally managed to obtain a berth on a ship that was apparently more to their taste than the *Caswell* (and her captain) had been. This was a grim harbinger of the travails yet to come for Captain 'Bully Best' and his ship.

This unexpected development meant that Captain Best was not only faced with obtaining a contract for a cargo in Buenos Aires but that he also needed to acquire almost an entirely new crew to work the ship back home. These matters typically took time to resolve and it would be six full weeks before the *Caswell* was ready to depart from Buenos Aires, her new crew in place.

Of the 'old' crew only Captain Best, William Wilson (first mate), Allan McLean (second mate), Peter MacGregor (carpenter), Charles McDonald and Walter Ferguson (apprentices) commenced the return journey. The steward's post was filled at Buenos Aires by Emmanuel Griffiths, a nineteen-year-old black Welshman, while the captain also selected two Maltese brothers (Gaspard and Joseph Pistoria), two British men (James Carrick and John Dunne), and Michael Rourke, who was Irish. A German cook named Rook Agineau was also taken on, as was a Greek seaman called Christos Emmanuel Bombos. For some reason (perhaps he was busy in trying to secure a cargo) the captain asked Bombos to find two more men to complete the crew and thus it was that George Peno a Turkish-Greek sailor (known as 'Big George') and Nicholas Morellos (another Turkish-Greek) came on board. This made sixteen men in all; not as many as on the outbound journey, but enough to get the ship home safely.

These appointments did not meet with universal acclaim, however. It seems that the newly recruited British contingent were unhappy at finding out that they were expected to serve with Maltese and Turkish-Greek crew members. This may simply have been the result of the racial attitudes prevailing at the time, or perhaps the British doubted whether the seafaring skills of the new recruits were sufficient for the potentially dangerous voyage home. In any event Carrick, Dunne and Rourke simply refused to sail and, when instructed to do so by Captain Best, instead demanded that they be allowed to see the British Consul on land to air their grievances. In response Captain Best – clearly not a man who took challenges to his authority lightly – simply cracked his baton over the head of Dunne before having all three placed in irons for several days. The consul need not be troubled.

While he now had a crew Best was still short of a cargo. The *Caswell* therefore left Buenos Aires on 23 October 1875 and sailed for the port of Valparaiso, rounding Cape Horn in the process. Captain Best allegedly worked his men hard during the voyage, as was his custom, probably adding to any unrest that existed on board. The *Caswell* arrived in port on 1 December 1875 and remained for three days, during which time Rourke, and the German cook, Agineau, both jumped ship. Agineau subsequently reported Best's behaviour to the British Consul but it seems that no action was taken. It would, after all, have been the word of a mere foreign cook against that of a British sea captain. Clearly that would be a 'no contest' so no further enquiry was deemed necessary on the part of the Consul.

With the elusive cargo seeming no nearer, the *Caswell* next up anchored and sailed to Antofogasta and here, finally, a deal was struck that would see the ship laden with saltpetre. At about this time (according to Bombos) it seems that the second mate, McLean, for some reason playing on tensions between the crew and the captain, told Joseph Pistoria that Best planned to kill the foreign crew members and pitch their bodies overboard. Pistoria, who spoke some English, later overheard the captain talking to other English captains that he had invited on board for dinner. Whether Pistoria, with his limited English, was misinterpreting or misunderstanding these discussions is unknown; but what he heard apparently confirmed – in Pistoria's mind at least – what McLean had told him earlier. He naturally shared this frightening information with his fellow sailors, raising the tension amongst the hard-worked crew to even higher levels.

It is very unlikely that Best would have sought to pursue the course of action that McLean had spoken of and Pistoria had now – possibly mistakenly – confirmed. It is hard to see what benefit such a murderous action would bring to the captain. As well as facing a probable charge of murder he would also have to bring home the ship with a much reduced crew, thus risking both it and its precious cargo (the saltpetre was valued at about £10,000 in its own right) not to mention the lives of those left on board. It is also hard to see what game McLean was up to by imparting such pro-vocative information to his fellow sailors.

On 1 January 1876 the *Caswell* slipped her mooring at Anto-fogasta and sailed first for Queenstown, Ireland, en route to Bristol where the saltpetre would be discharged. On the following Sunday Christos Bombos lay sick in his bunk and was unable to undertake his watch duty. Wilson, the first mate, ordered 'Big George' (George Peno) to act as a substitute but was promptly rebuffed by Peno who felt that his poor English would be a hindrance rather than a help on a watch that was already primarily composed of non-English speakers. It would also mean him completing two turns at watch which he regarded as unfair. Wilson repeated his instruction, adding that in the event of non-compliance he would tell the captain. Peno stood his ground and made no movement.

Captain Best arrived shortly afterwards with Wilson in tow. Best was brandishing a revolver and ordered Peno to take up his posi-tion under the muzzle of the gun. Peno still refused, pointing out that typically in such cases the captain should endorse the ship's log and place the miscreant in irons for the remainder of the journey rather than wave a gun around. He had no objection to being so placed in irons. The captain, his bluff having been called, retired on Peno's promise to complete the ten o'clock watch if Bombos was still indisposed. In the event it seems that, despite Bombos not being fit, Peno did not show up and the watch went ahead one man short.

On the morning of 4 January 1876 Big George was working on the ship's rigging when Captain Best left his cabin and immedi-ately engaged him in conversation. Possibly Best was challenging Peno on his non-attendance on watch and his general demeanour, but onlookers at the time were unable to hear exactly what was said. Whatever it was it had a galvanising effect on Peno who – already holding a knife for the task he was engaged in – struck the captain with two slashing blows to his abdomen, almost in the shape of a cross. While the captain cried out 'My God! My God!' his intestines burst out through the wounds. Best then stood there momentarily, staring in horror and disbelief at the entrails he was now holding in his hands. At that moment Joseph Pistoria leapt forward from the ship's wheel and shot Best twice in the head, the gun being so close to its victim that it left a blue mark on the captain's ear. Best slumped to the deck, still clutching his pro-truding intestines to his body.

First Mate William Wilson witnessed the attack on the captain and ran towards the rear of the ship, probably to get a weapon with which to defend himself. He was intercepted on the way by Nicholas Morellos who stabbed him twice before being joined by Peno who added two further blows with the knife he had wielded to such deadly effect on the captain. If that was not enough Joseph Pistoria also approached the stricken man and shot him despite Wilson's anguished pleas of 'Not me Joseph!'

The black steward, Emmanuel Griffiths, was in the cabin when the attacks started but he came nervously up the stairway to the deck when summoned by Peno and Pistoria. As he reached the top he was shot three times by Pistoria but, though wounded, continued to try and avoid his attackers. Finally cornered by Peno, he was dragged to the cabin and ordered to reveal where the ship's weapons were kept. With that done Peno mounted a furious attack on the steward with his knife; indeed, his appetite for violence was not sated until he had cut out a part of his victim's heart and thrown it on the deck. Gaspard Pistoria also shot Griffiths in the head though by that time it can have had no real harmful effect; the steward was already dead.

Allan McLean had run into the deckhouse and tried to prevent the entry of others. However, with door and window being attacked by the mutineers he realised the ultimate futility of his situation and – with the desperation of a doomed man – he quickly left the cabin and ran down the poop deck stairs to a lower deck. He was soon felled by a combination of shots and stabs, with Peno delivering what seemed to be the decisive blows with his knife. He fell to the deck near to where his captain lay.

After this outburst of sustained violence matters seemed to calm down a little. The carpenter, MacGregor, was put in fear of his life and was – kneeling in the blood of his captain – made to swear fealty to the mutineers. But he came to no harm as was also the case with Carrick, who emerged from his hiding place in a coal bunker having been reassured that as a simple seaman he was safe. MacDonald and Ferguson, the young apprentices, were also left unharmed.

The four stricken men were laid out on deck and a rope was attached to their feet and then they were all secured to an anchor. This was heaved over the side of the ship, bodies and all, in the expectation that all would sink. It was noted that at this time that the captain still showed signs of life and was still trying to contain his intestines. Similarly, the second mate showed signs of movement. Any hopes that the sea would quickly swallow the mutineers' grim handiwork were dashed when the bodies separated from the anchor and floated away. Their chance of discovery and rescue on the open sea was, of course, negligible.

It is hard to tell whether the mutiny was pre-planned and signalled by Big George's savage attack on Captain Best, or whether it was unplanned and followed Best's unheard retorts to Big George which seemingly tipped the mariner over the edge for some unknown reason. In any event it was now the foreign crew contingent that was giving the orders and the decks were soon being swabbed of blood (including the steward's heart) while Carrick who – unlike the mutineers – could navigate the ship was told to check the ship's position. The ship's name was also painted over and any small equipment or utensils that bore its name were thrown overboard though the forecastle bell seems to have been overlooked in the rush.

The other conundrum for the British was whether the mutineers were acting solely against the rule of a tyrannical captain and those closely associated with him, or against the rest of the crew in general? Certainly, the captain and his officers together with the steward had all been killed, leaving only plain seamen on board. Those who had not attempted to prevent the mutiny might have so acted due to a disinterest in the fate of a harsh captain or simply due to a fear of getting too involved in a very dangerous situation. With the mutiny seen to be a success the question for the non-foreign contingent was: were they still safe in the company of their bloody-handed crew mates?

Another concern was what did the mutineers plan to do with the *Caswell*? They were now short-handed on crew members and lacked the navigational skills necessary to steer to a destination without Carrick's assistance. There was talk of a return to Buenos Aires where the foreigners would go ashore and vanish into the crowd, leaving the ship in the possession of the British. An added attraction of that option was that Gaspard Pistoria's wife lived there, and the two brothers intimated that they would leave ship at that point, regardless of any longer term plans for the *Caswell* and its crew. Another discussion amongst the mutineers apparently centred on the idea of murdering the British, scuttling the ship and going ashore as the survivors of a ship wreck, with all evidence of their foul deeds hidden in the depths of the sea.

The Pistoria brothers duly left the *Caswell* at Buenos Aires in late February 1876, taking with them a letter written by Carrick (probably under duress) that exonerated them from any part in the mutiny. Nicholas Morellos now assumed command and it became apparent that the *Caswell* was to be sailed into Greek waters and their longer term objective was to be the island of Samos in the Mediterranean. Rumours reached the British (the mutineers seemed to distrust each other and some shared their concerns with the British) that they would be butchered, the ship sunk and any remaining valuables and equipment would be 'laundered' through a Greek shipping agent. This was unsettling news and it became apparent to the British crew members that if they were to complete the voyage safely they might well need to take decisive action on their own account in the near future.

On the night of 11 March 1876 Big George Peno was supposedly keeping watch from the poop deck. He was possibly drunk. At about 2.00 am Peter MacGregor, the carpenter, entered the forecastle where the British slept and simply said 'Now boys, for your lives . . .' At this MacGregor, Dunne and Carrick, armed with ship's tools that included an axe and an adze, made their way onto deck and towards Peno. On assessing the situation – Peno was alone – Dunne pointedly pulled his cap onto his head. This was the pre-arranged signal between the counter-mutineers. There was to be no turning back now. On seeing the men approach and perceiving their intent Peno advanced boldly with his knife in his hand. As he lunged forward he was struck heavily on the head with the axe by MacGregor and fell senseless onto the deck.

A noise from below deck then caused MacGregor and Carrick to descend the companion way and confront Bombos and Morellos in the state room. While Carrick attacked Bombos, MacGregor first had to dodge several shots fired by Morellos before Carrick managed to assist his crewmate by giving the Greek a hard 'lick' with the axe, almost severing his head and immediately ending his resistance. As the wounded Bombos was dragged onto deck it was noticed that the groggy Peno was attempting to rise, still clutching his knife. Dunne acted resolutely by grasping the axe from Carrick's trembling hands and striking several decisive blows that split Big George's skull in three places. The counter-mutiny had succeeded.

With the ship now secure, albeit in the midst of a dangerous sea, there was no option other than to try and sail an under-manned

Montage of the Caswell *Mutiny. James Carrick (top left); the* Caswell *under tow off Queenstown (bottom left); Cork Gaol (top right); Christos Bombos in the dock (middle right); Christos Bombos in custody (bottom right).* Mary Evans Picture Library

vessel to a port of safety. Clearly not a man who was easily daunted Carrick, who assumed command due to his navigational skills, set sail for Queenstown in Ireland. He would bring home the *Caswell*, its surviving crew, the prisoner and the valuable cargo.

After a further two months at sea the *Caswell* finally arrived at Kinsale on 13 May 1876 where she was met by the *Goshawk* and taken into tow. The ship and its occupants became the centre of intense interest as local people crowded round to catch a glimpse of the heroic crew members and their prisoner. The vessel's owners were, of course, concerned about the *Caswell* as well as its crew and the vessel was speedily moved to Bristol in order that its valuable cargo could be discharged. Similar excitement was shown at Bristol where the press of people on the dockside became so great that the authorities started charging sixpence per person to board the ship and view the scene of the terrible crimes. The sights included bullet holes in the wood as well as the mark of a hatchet stroke. Proceeds were to be devoted to a fund set up for the widow and five children of the unfortunate first mate, Wilson.

Following the formality of committal proceedings Christos Emmanuel Bombos appeared for trial on a charge of murder in the Cork Criminal Court on 27 July 1876. He was accused of stabbing both the captain and second mate and generally assisting the other mutineers in their murderous intentions. Bombos was described as being about five feet and six inches in height, of dark complexion and hair, his face distinguished by a cataract over his left eye through which he could not see. Translation of the evidence for Bombos's benefit was undertaken by Mr Cartwright, though for some unexplained reason Bombos's own counsel stopped this assistance periodically, leaving Bombos very much in the dark as the trial progressed.

A small procession of witnesses provided compelling evidence that was very much to the detriment of Bombos. The thrust of Bombos's defence was that he had not struck any blows with a knife on anyone. Additionally any assistance that he had given to the mutiny had been driven by threats against Bombos made by Big George. His claim of not having wielded a knife was contradicted by witnesses and the court allowed him little leeway on his claim of acting under duress. He also claimed to have forewarned the British about plans to do away with them that were being hatched by the others.

Another of the contentions made by Bombos was that the counter-mutiny had been almost as vicious as the original mutiny. He claimed that Big George was, in all probability, asleep when set on with an axe. Similarly he claimed that Morellos had been asleep when he was decapitated and that he, Bombos, had been summarily woken from his slumbers by an axe blow to the head. Contrary to the claims of the British that there had been resistance to the counter-mutiny the truth, according to Bombos, was that the original mutineers had been killed as they slept. No effort had been made to secure them and bring them to the justice of a court of law (himself excepted, of course). The evidence from the British crew members flatly contradicted that of Bombos and Carrick simply claimed to have been acting in self defence.

Bombos also gave evidence of the ill treatment of crew members by Captain Best and this pattern of abuse had been borne out by the earlier actions of many of the original Scottish crew who declined to sign on the *Caswell* for the return journey from South America. Two members of the new crew had also jumped ship at the first opportunity. Indeed, further information that supported Bombos's view of Captain Best (though it arrived by letter and after the trial had finished) came from Edward Warner of Birmingham who had served with Best aboard the *William Leckie* in 1864. Warner recalled Best treating his steward '. . . inhumanly and brutally . . .' on one occasion beating his face with a thick rope until the blood ran onto the deck and on another lashing him in chains to a beam and allowing him to painfully swing there for twenty minutes. It was apparently common practice for Best to wave a pistol in the face of a crew member, threatening to put a hole through him were it not for the law preventing him. In the light of this confirmatory evidence perhaps Best's nickname of 'Bully' was well deserved.

Of course it was not the late captain who was on trial in Cork and the defence seemed to act on the slim hope that the jury might see the provocative actions of the captain as justification for returning a verdict of manslaughter rather than murder. When the judge summed up he immediately knocked away the props that feebly supported Bombos's defence. The jurors should, he stated, confine their deliberations to what happened on the 4 January 1876, the day of the mutiny. What the captain had done prior to that date was irrelevant. Whatever it was it did not justify a deadly attack on the captain and several members of his crew. What was done during the counter-mutiny should also have no influence on what had happened on the 4 January. Similarly, even if Bombos had played only a small part in the mutiny, not striking any blows himself as he claimed, the mere fact that he assisted the murderous members of the crew made him as guilty as the man who had struck a fatal blow. Finally the judge rebuked the defence counsel for even suggesting that the jury might substitute a finding of manslaughter in place of the actual charge of wilful murder. It was to be a finding of guilty or innocent of murder, with no shade of opinion in between.

The jury then retired to commence its deliberations. After almost three hours they reported back that they were at an impasse with eleven members reaching a finding of guilty whilst the twelfth member found Bombos innocent. Asked to meet again and see if the twelfth juror could be persuaded by reasoned argument to the view of the majority they returned again after a further two hours had elapsed. There had been no change in their situation and the judge had no option other than to reluctantly discharge them. The Crown representatives immediately asked that the case be retried before a fresh jury on the following Monday and when the defence pointed out that some of its witnesses would not be available the judge cuttingly remarked that 'You did not produce a witness that proved anything'. The case would indeed proceed afresh on Monday, with or without the absent witnesses.

With a new jury sworn in the case proceeded much in the way of the previous weeks' trial. There were no surprises in the evidence and the jury duly retired, the judge no doubt hoping for a firm decision on this occasion. He was not to be disappointed; after a retirement of only an hour the jury returned to record a verdict of 'guilty'. When asked whether he had anything to say before sentence was passed Bombos declared via his interpreter:

Yes, I have. Before my God and my country I declare that I am innocent of the crime imputed to me. At the time that I held one of the mates against the rail, I did it from fear and compulsion of 'George', who threatened my life with a knife. I deny that I committed the crime on the vessel. On the contrary I did my best to save the English crew, the cargo, and the ship. That is all I have to say, and I declare that before my God, my Saviour and Redeemer. I did not strike anyone with my knife at all.

Sentence of death by hanging was then passed and the prisoner taken down. Despite several attempts by parties sympathetic to the plight of Bombos to gain a reprieve it was decided that the law must run its course. Bombos, apparently realising that there was to be no last minute reprieve, paid great attention to his spiritual welfare and received a number of local priests as well as those of the Greek church at Liverpool as he awaited the day of execution. He was to be executed in a double hanging, the other unfortunate being Thomas Crowe, who was to hang for a politically motivated murder.

So it was that on 25 August 1876 Bombos made his final preparations at the Cork County Gaol. He slept fitfully from around midnight on the 24 August but was awake at four o'clock on the

25th at which time he resumed his prayers. He smoked but took no breakfast. At ten to eight he left in procession (behind Crowe and his attendants) for what was a long walk of over 300 yards to the prison airing yard where the gallows had been erected. This was an iron frame that could be raised and lowered by means of a windlass. Two hooks were placed on top of the crossbar and from these would dangle the hangman's ropes, each ending in a noose.

William Marwood, public executioner was credited with a more scientific approach to calculating the drop necessary to break a man's neck, thus avoiding a slow strangulation. In an eleven year career he hanged almost 200 people. Paul Townsend

Bombos was accompanied by an Archimandrite of the Greek Church and his two assistants, the Rev J Q Connolly, and two warders. Waiting in the yard were seven reporters, two doctors and three warders. Another warder, positioned on the central tower of the prison, raised his hat as a signal to this waiting group that the procession was approaching. It was heard before it was seen – Crowe's pleas of 'Lord have mercy on me!' being repeated unceasingly. At the rear of the procession the exhortations of the Greek priest were answered in kind by Bombos, who strode unflinchingly forward. As Crowe paused at the entrance to the execution yard he was suddenly confronted by Marwood, the public executioner, who quickly eyed up his reluctant client and promptly loosened Crowe's black scarf, so as to expose the neck. 'Lord have mercy on me!' intoned the crestfallen Crowe.

Marwood then turned his attention to Bombos, pinioning his arms before Crowe was led into the yard with the Greek six paces behind him. With Crowe having already ascended the platform Bombos for a moment recoiled at the stairs and stared gloomily at the stark apparatus of death that now loomed over him. Quickly recovering his composure he followed his Greek priest up to the platform. Marwood, attired in a black body coat and a light tweed trouser, then placed both men on the drop while the convicted and their clergy prayed constantly. While Crowe was given the sign of the cross by the Rev McNamara, The Greek Archimandrite kissed Bombos who responded in turn by kissing the priest's hand. This being completed Marwood made his final adjustments to the ropes and placed caps over the men's heads before quickly releasing the bolt.

The drop had been set at eight feet and it killed Crowe instantly. Indeed, the red handkerchief that he had clasped lightly in his hand remained so positioned even as his body swung beneath the scaffold. The white cap, however, had been dislodged in the fall and Marwood hastily scrambled beneath the platform to replace it and thus spare the onlookers a sight of a presumably anguished face. It was not so easy for Bombos. The fall did not kill him outright and he continued to jerk spasmodically for around four minutes before his body too finally fell still.

Before his walk to the scaffold Bombos had made a final statement that had been written down by his interpreter. In it he again denied any guilt in the crimes of which he had been convicted. He expressed his gratitude to the clergy – both Catholic and Greek – who had supported him in the dark days before the day of execution and also thanked the prison governor. A silver crucifix presented to the Archimandrite by two local ladies, and used in his ministrations to Bombos, was to be forwarded to his mother in Athens after his death. Finally, he forgave all who had given evidence against him and said that he hoped to be similarly forgiven by a merciful God.

And there the tragic story of the Swansea based *Caswell* might have ended was it not for a chance encounter in Montevideo in January 1879, two and a half years after the execution of Bombos. The survivors of the mutiny had naturally had to rebuild their lives and for a number of them the only thing they really knew was the sea. One such man was James Carrick, seen as the hero of the counter-mutiny by many. In January 1879 he was in Montevideo, having secured a contract to ship bird guano from a remote island off the coast of Patagonia back to Britain. Sitting in a café one day he momentarily glimpsed someone who he was sure was one of the Pistoria brothers. He remained calmly at his seat being anxious not to give the game away by over-reacting. When he again nonchalantly glanced across to where the suspect had been he was dismayed to see that the man had vanished.

Fate had not finished with Carrick and the Pistoria's, however. A week later Carrick was astounded to not only see Joseph Pistoria reappear, but also to find that they were to – once again – serve on board the same ship! They were both aboard the German barque *Maria* and while Carrick carefully avoided direct contact with his old shipmate it soon became apparent that, in any event, Pistoria did not remember him. Carrick then wasted no time in summoning the assistance of the consular authorities and Pistoria – who offered no resistance – was taken into custody. Of his brother there was no sign.

Pistoria was shipped back to Britain, arriving in late March 1879, and was then handed over to the authorities in Cork to be duly brought up for trial. The trial began on 22 July 1879 and, bearing in mind that Joseph Pistoria had allegedly played a more prominent role in the mutiny than the executed Bombos, there can have been little doubt as to the eventual outcome. A verdict of 'guilty' was duly brought in and the date of execution was set for 25 August 1879 – three years to the day that fellow mutineer Bombos had been pitched into eternity. Realising that he needed to get his affairs into order for the benefit of his remaining family Pistoria admitted to the Italian Consul that he was actually Francesco Moschara, a native of Sicily rather than Malta, and was thirty-seven years old. As in the case of Bombos, well intentioned appeals for clemency came to nothing and the execution was duly carried out on 25 August 1879.

Gaspard Pistoria (or Moschara) was never traced so the execution of his brother Joseph marked the last chapter in the *Caswell* tragedy. In all, it had cost the lives of four crew members and four mutineers. Even today the real reasons behind the mutiny remain clouded in mystery, the evidence of the prosecution witnesses flatly contradicting that of the accused. Why had some of the British been clapped in irons before the return journey commenced? Just how well did 'Bully Best' live up to his name on the voyage? Was that sufficient justification for a tyrannised crew to strike back, albeit with appalling violence? Had the British cynically incited the foreigners to take a course of action against a bully that they themselves shrank back from? And then later aligned their evidence so as to ensure the conviction of their shipmates? We will, of course, never know.

And what became of the barque *Caswell* itself? This unhappy ship naturally continued to ply its trade for the benefit of its

Swansea based owners. It had, after all, been newly built at considerable expense at the time of the 1876 mutiny, and was fitted
with every modern appliance. A healthy return on such an invest-
ment was clearly required. On 18 February 1899 it set sail from
New South Wales with a cargo of coal and a crew of twelve. It was
never seen again.

CHAPTER 11

Suffer Little Children: Thomas Nash and His Daughter
1885

I am praying and asking God for mercy and forgiveness for all my sins.

The evening of 4 December 1885 was a stormy one, with a high wind blowing. On the seafront at Swansea a heavy sea pounded the beach and the larger waves occasionally broke over the dark mass of the west pier. Thomas Fender, a boatman, standing at the door of the watch house was surprised to see a man walking towards the pier in the company of a young female child. The couple duly walked onto the pier and were soon lost from sight.

Given the lateness of the hour and the prevailing weather the pier was deserted. Fender pondered over what could cause a man to go onto the pier in such conditions, and with a child in tow. George Pritchard, an assistant pilot at the port, had followed after the couple but had soon lost sight of them in the gloom. He had then returned to the boat house, where he was due to shortly pay out some money. A little later Fender was surprised to see a man coming off the pier alone. He concluded that this must be the man he had seen earlier and, noting the absence of the child, his suspicions were immediately aroused. This suspicion seemed to somehow make itself known to the man on the pier who promptly jumped over the side and onto the sands, an alarming drop of about fourteen feet. Fender set off in pursuit in the company of a companion, William Owen, who was another assistant pilot at the port.

They duly apprehended the stranger and demanded to be told where the young girl was. Answers to their questions, however, were only obtained with difficulty. However, he eventually claimed that she was '. . . on the top . . .' of the pier before admitting that she was, in fact, underneath the pier. Whilst it was possible to walk underneath the top level decking of the pier, to do so on such a night was to invite danger. The fact that the person placed in this dangerous predicament was a five-year-old child was even more alarming.

On receipt of this chilling news Fender and Owen escorted the man up to the boat house and into the custody of the hastily summoned police. Police Constable Payne conducted a speedy search of the foreshore and the pier itself but to no avail. Returning with a large lamp he searched for a further fifteen minutes before discovering the body of a child. This was about sixteen yards from the pier and about ten yards from the high water mark. The child was clearly dead and was partially buried in the sand. The body was subsequently examined by Mr Thomas, a local surgeon, who found no bruising on the body and confirmed drowning as the cause of death.

The man in custody was Thomas Nash, who was employed as a labourer by the Swansea Corporation. He was thirty-nine years old and a widower, who stood at five feet and seven inches, with brown hair. He lived at Graham Street, in the Hafod area of the town. The deceased was later discovered to be Martha Ann, his five-year-old daughter. What could have driven a father to apparently show such murderous cruelty to his own child? A very sad tale would soon be recounted at the coroner's inquest into the death and Thomas Nash's subsequent trial for wilful murder at the Glamorgan Assizes. The trial took place in February 1886.

Before that it was, of course, necessary for the funeral of poor little Martha Ann to take place. With the child's mother already deceased, her father in prison, and only an older sister still surviving (but not yet herself an adult), it was understandable that family money to pay for a funeral was in short supply.

A police bulls eye lantern. These had a small oil reservoir with a wick, and a shield that could block out the light when required. The light emitted was in any event poor. South Wales Police Museum

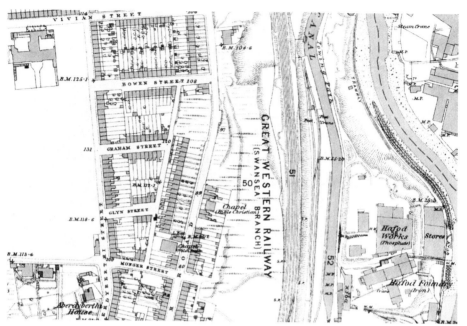

Map showing the location of Graham Street in the Hafod area of Swansea. West Glamorgan Archive Service

However, thanks to the kindness and generosity of the people of Hafod and Plasmarl, the late child's neighbourhood, a collection was arranged. Martha Ann's body had lain at the mortuary and it was anticipated that a pauper funeral would be required. However, neighbours Mrs Miles and Mrs Boys soon obtained enough funds to pay for a church burial. Another neighbour, Mrs Davies, accepted the body into her home prior to the funeral service, where it was viewed with great sadness by dozens of Martha Ann's former playmates.

In due course the body was conveyed in solemn procession to the Llangyfelach churchyard, where her mother already lay at rest, followed by a large and mournful crowd. The procession was led by the English Baptist Band of Hope, of which Martha Ann had been a member in happier times. The only relative present at the interment was Sarah, the elder daughter of Thomas Nash and Martha Ann's big sister. The hymn *Safe in the Arms of Jesus* was sung most affectingly, as was *It is well with my Soul* before the interment took place before a hushed assembly. Thus closed the last chapter in an innocent life so cruelly cut short.

Thomas Nash's wife had died some five years before the tragic death of his youngest daughter. He had lived with Martha Ann, who would have been six in January 1886, and his elder daughter, Sarah, who was seventeen. They lived at the Plasmarl home of a Mrs Goodwin, who took in respectable men (and their families) as lodgers. He had informed his children that he planned to remarry but had not told them to whom, or when this would happen. This was naturally a cause for concern to his children but Nash had assured them that he would take apartments in the Morriston area of the town, where they could join him and his new wife. Sarah Nash observed that her father, who was generally a quiet man, had recently taken to staying out late and drinking heavily. Mrs Goodwin confirmed that Nash was quiet and steady and was a kind, and somewhat indulgent father, to his children.

Rumours of the new marriage had also reached the ears of Mrs Goodwin, who was keen to discover how much longer he might remain as her paying lodger. Encountering Nash in the street one day (at this time he did not apparently sleep at his lodgings every night) she questioned him on the issue, as well as whether she was to continue to keep and feed his children. The question of out-standing payment for the children's food and lodgings also arose. Nash asked that Martha Ann be kept until the following Friday, when he would collect her. However, Nash failed to appear then and on several other occasions, despite Mrs Goodwin threatening to present the children at the Swansea Workhouse, if payment remained outstanding.

Another witness, Hannah Duffy, told the court that Nash had in fact come to lodge with her on 17 November 1885, accompanied by his new wife. There they remained until the events of the 4 December. At no time did Duffy hear Nash or his new wife refer to the existence of children from an earlier marriage. It is apparent that during this period Nash's children remained at the home of Mrs Goodwin and, as it turned out, his new wife was simply un-aware of their existence.

Her patience finally exhausted, Mrs Goodwin had visited the Corporation pay office on Friday 4 December 1885 where, in due course, Nash appeared to collect his weekly wage. She presented him with her final bill (in the sum of £1-16s-2d), as well as Martha Ann, who had accompanied her. Once again Nash promised to pay, but this time on the following day. At this little Martha Ann enquired 'Shall I come home with you, Mrs Goodwin', to which

Mrs Goodwin replied 'No my dear, you must go with your father'. No one at the time could have reasonably foreseen the awful consequences of this brief conversation. After this encounter Nash was seen by a workmate to leave with the child and head towards the pier area, in the opposite direction to his new lodgings with Hannah Duffy in the Hafod.

At his trial Nash claimed that he had walked onto the pier and placed his daughter on the wooden rail of the pier prior to lifting her onto his back, so that he could carry her more easily, Martha Ann being tired. A high gust of wind had then blown her off the rail and into the sea. A contention by Nash that he had earlier claimed that she 'had dropped' – adding credence to his claim – rather than she was 'on the top', was refuted by witness Thomas Fender. The wind direction on the night would have tended to keep the girl on the pier, rather than blow her off it, commented Fender. Medical evidence had also revealed no bruising on the body, which was strange if the claim that she had fallen off a rail was true. The implication of this evidence was that Martha Ann had avoided all obstacles as she fell into the water. In short, it was probable that she had been forcibly thrown from the pier edge into deeper water.

With all the evidence having been submitted, Mr Glascodine, for the defence, emphasised the heavy burden that now rested on the jury. If there was any bias on the part of the jury then it must be given up in the favour of the prisoner. His client had lived a quiet life and was kind and loving towards his children. No-one had witnessed what had transpired on the pier between Nash and his daughter, but it was unreasonable to assume that his known parental fondness could have vanished in one, dark minute and led to the murder of little Martha Ann.

The action of the accused in apparently trying to flee the scene and then being reticent in answering questions could be merely the result of his having undergone a traumatic experience. His mind might have simply become unhinged and his reasoning temporarily impaired. A sudden drop in wind speed and the ensuing lack of resistance of a body braced against it might have been enough to cause Martha Ann to tumble into the sea. The body of a well fed child, cushioned by layers of clothing on a stormy night, might not show the bruising that would otherwise be occasioned by such a fall. The defence also claimed that Nash's real expression on the night was 'She has slipped off', but – it was claimed – this was misinterpreted by excited witnesses, in a dramatic situation, and at the height of a noisy storm.

The judge – who in this case was the Lord Chief Justice of England – then summed up the case, carefully distinguishing between the possible verdicts of murder, manslaughter, or not guilty. The fact that there were no first hand witnesses to the tragic final moments of little Martha Ann's life did not mean that a verdict of not guilty was necessarily appropriate. The weight of circumstantial evidence might lead the jury to conclude that there was no reasonable possibility that someone else had committed the crime, were the incident not thought to be merely a tragic accident. The judge referred to the unusual circumstance of Nash taking his daughter onto the pier on a stormy night. To do this he had also headed off in the opposite direction of his new lodgings. His subsequent behaviour had attracted the attention of several witnesses whose suspicions had been aroused to the extent that they had wasted no time in apprehending him. These facts needed the careful consideration of the jury.

The question of motive might also not appear to be clear to the jury members in the case before them. This was of no concern. No motive was sufficient to justify the crime of murder, and it was only God who could see the inner secrets of men's hearts. It might be that the prisoner saw his younger daughter as a possible burden to him and his new wife, but this was pure supposition. Indeed, there were other cases where lesser motives than this had led to murder.

Thomas Nash who repented his sins when faced with the hangman. Media Wales *The Western Mail*

His summing up concluded, the jury retired to consider their verdict, taking with them plans of the harbour and its piers. It seems that the evidence presented by the prosecution and its witnesses had been quite compelling. After a retirement of only fifteen minutes the jury returned to deliver a verdict of guilty of wilful murder. At this Nash, who had sat with his chin on his chest and his

THE SWANSEA CHILD MURDER.

hands clasped before him, taking little obvious interest in the proceedings, broke out into a sudden sweat. Asked if he had anything to say before sentence was duly passed he merely exclaimed 'I am not guilty'.

The Lord Chief Justice then moved to place the dreaded black cap onto his head. It was noted that his hand trembled as he did so. As the words of the death sentence were pronounced, with great solemnity, several jurors were seen to be visibly affected, while muffled sobs arose from the public gallery. Outside the court Nash's surviving daughter, Sarah, was seen to be convulsed by agonised weeping. With her mother dead and having lost her little sister in the most tragic of circumstances, she now faced the grim prospect of losing her father as well, though many would have argued that his appointment with the public executioner was well deserved.

The date of execution was set for Monday, 1 March 1886 and attempts by well intentioned citizens to have Nash's sentence reduced to one of penal servitude came to nought. It was reported that the prisoner had suffered no loss of appetite during his incarceration, sometimes taking a pint of soup in addition to the ordinary prison diet. However, if his appetite remained healthy until the end, the same cannot be said of his conscience. It is apparent that as he awaited his fateful meeting with James Berry, the public executioner, the great weight of his evil crime bore heavily upon him. Rumours had also reached him that the people of Swansea thought him unrepentant of his awful crime. To correct this false impression he wrote several letters just days before his execution, one of which (dated 27 February 1886 and with minor spelling mistakes corrected by the author) was published in the *Western Mail*. It read (with not a little eloquence):

> *Dear Friends – I write these few lines for you to have them published in the paper for to let the public at large know what has been put in the papers about my life since my conviction has all been false, for I have paid every attention to the chaplain, and have confessed everything to him, and I am praying and asking God for mercy and forgiveness for all my sins, and for that murder that I committed . . . one of the most awful and cruel crimes as could be committed on my dear daughter, Martha Ann Nash, and God has heard my prayers, and He in His tender mercy has answered them, and He has taken all my sins on Him, and I am become a new man, a vile sinner washed in the blood of*

Jesus Christ by believing and trusting in His holy word – that word which says 'Whosoever believeth in the Son hath everlasting life,' and I am glad to tell you all that I shall on Monday morning, the day of my execution, depart in peace and be forever with Jesus and with Martha Ann, where there is no more trouble and sorrow nor no sin can enter there, and I hope I shall see my other daughter, Sarah, up there at the right hand of Christ, who shall be our judge on the great Judgement Day, when He will be sifting the good out from the wicked. Dear readers and hearers of the papers, I should like to inform you and let you know I am quite pleased with Mr. Glascodine, who was defending my case, and also to the others that had to do with the case, for the sentence that was passed on me was only what I really did deserve, for I did do it wilfully, and I am happy to tell you all that I can die in the Lord a happy sinner, with all my sins washed in the blood of the Lamb. Dear friends, I would sooner die in the Lord on Monday morning than to have to reprieve and live in misery all the days of my life, and after all lose Christ, and be lost for ever . . . No more troubles, no more trials in this world, but in the world to come there will be gladness and rejoicing over sinners that repenteth . . .

Nash ended the letter by thanking the prison officials and chaplain for their kindness since being imprisoned.

Swansea awoke on 1 March 1886 to a covering of snow which was up to a foot deep in parts. The wind was cold and the town looked bleak and miserable. As 8.00 am neared, a crowd of over 4,000 people thronged outside the prison. The night had passed without incident for Nash who, after a hearty breakfast, was now having a final meeting with Mr Hudson, the prison chaplain. At the conclusion of this meeting his arms were securely strapped and he was led out of the cell, executioner Berry taking him by the arm on one side, and Chief Warder Box gripping the other. The chaplain led the solemn procession whilst reciting the burial service, followed by the High Sheriff, Under Sheriff, prison surgeon and the governor, plus several representatives of the media.

The group then approached the deadly apparatus of execution, which had been brought from Birmingham jail, and appeared to be incapable of failure such was the simplicity of its trapdoor mechanism. Once under the beam Berry quickly pinioned the condemned man's legs while Nash stood firmly to attention, only a troubled sigh revealing any hint of anxiety. The white hood was duly placed over his head and the noose adjusted. No sooner had Nash managed to exclaim, in a subdued voice, 'Lord have mercy upon my soul' than Berry, with the speed of a man who knew what he was about, pushed the lever and released the trap. The body dropped a short distance below the surface of the platform, where it swayed, but showed no sign of a struggle. Death – caused by dislocation of the neck – was adjudged to have been instantaneous. Indeed, Nash's hands – which had been clasped when he was placed on the trap – were found to be still clasped when his body was cut down an hour later.

James Berry, Public Executioner. In an eight year career he hanged around 130 people and later wrote his memoirs, the first executioner to do so. Paul Townsend

The simple fact of the case was that – for reasons beyond our comprehension – Nash had omitted to tell his new wife that he had two daughters from his earlier marriage. Presumably, he had hoped that the older Sarah could be left largely to her own devices, being of an age where employment was quite possible. Little Martha Ann, however, would have to be cared for by his new wife, an issue he had apparently not previously broached with her. Martha Ann, at only five years old, would therefore clearly be a cause of possible friction between Nash and his new wife. Tragically, it would seem that Nash saw a truly desperate and evil action as the only solution to his self-imposed predicament. How he planned to explain his daughter's death to Sarah and others we can only guess at.

Thus it was with the execution of Thomas Nash that a line was finally drawn under a most harrowing tale. One can only hope that the fervent prayers of a penitent sinner, to be reunited in peace with his ill-used daughter in heaven, were not left unanswered.

CHAPTER 12

Murder at the
Gloucester Hotel
1889

It was not my intention to cut
the gentleman.

t around midnight on a snowy 10 February 1889, Frederick George Kent, landlord of the *Gloucester Hotel*, Gloucester Place, Swansea, secured the doors to the premises and retired to his bedroom, taking with him the day's takings in a cashbox. Mrs Kent went with him and readied her-self for bed while Mr Kent had a bath and attended to his corns. The hotel was located in an area close to the docks at Swansea, and was a popular haunt of seafaring men of all nationalities. As was Mr Kent's custom, given that he habitually kept the hotel takings in a cashbox within the room, he locked the bedroom door as an additional security measure, before getting into bed himself.

Both slumbered peacefully. At about 5.30 am Mrs Kent was awoken by what sounded like a match being struck in the room. She discerned the shadowy figure of a man standing in the shadows and immediately woke her husband. Mr Kent leapt out of bed and closed with the stranger, whose facial features were indistinguishable in the gloom, the intruder having snuffed out the light he had momentarily lit. While Mr Kent struggled violently with the man Mrs Kent fumbled frantically beneath a pillow for her husband's revolver.

Finally grasping the handgun Mrs Kent then lit a candle and was able to see her husband grappling with a black man. In a desperate attempt to help her husband Mrs Kent fired a single shot which she was sure struck her husband's attacker. He fell to the floor and crawled under the bed only to quickly re-emerge and throw a large mirror at Mr Kent that fortunately missed its target. A further struggle ensued in which the light was again put out for a short

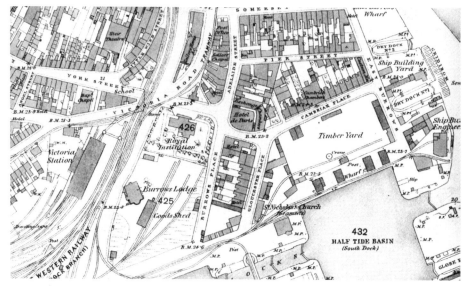

Gloucester Place, Swansea. The Gloucester Hotel *is to the left of St Nicholas Church.* West Glamorgan Archive Service

time before the man broke free, opened the door and fled the room.

Mrs Kent now attempted to hand her husband the revolver but was alarmed to see him staggering and bleeding heavily. He was unable to hold the gun and Mrs Kent helped him onto the bed. She then called for help and was assisted by two servants, one of whom shouted 'murder' through an opened window. Assistance arrived in the shape of Doctor Howell Thomas and Police Constable Cross. Mrs Kent herself discovered a bloodstained razor on the floor of the room that she knew was not her husband's. Also discovered were a hat and a pair of shoes that also did not belong to Mr Kent. At about 8.05 am, despite the urgent medical assistance given, Mr Kent expired.

Police Constable Cross went off in search of the assailant. He noticed that the back doors to the premises were open and there were tracks in the snow that led out of the hotel yard and along a lane. The tracks were not exactly in the form of shoe-prints, being a little more indistinct than those that would have been made by a semi-rigid shoe. It appeared that a wall had also been scaled and the tracks then went off in the direction of the South Dock, before the trail in the snow was lost amongst other, unconnected footprints. Assisted by officials of the harbour trust, Police Constable Cross visited several vessels moored in the dock but found no black men matching the description given by Mrs Kent.

In the meantime Detective Inspector David Jones had been called to the crime scene at about 6.30 am and, from enquiries made, had formed a strong suspicion as to who the culprit might be. With a visit to the suspect's lodgings revealing nothing a search was commenced in the docks area. At the South Dock, Edward Charles, an engine driver at the Globe Dock, was assisting in the search when he spotted a black man crouching under a fire grate. At the moment of discovery the man got up and presented himself peacefully to the policemen and other searchers who had surged towards him. The prime suspect in the crime had been swiftly apprehended.

Detective Gill handcuffed the suspect, who was wearing a light suit with white cuffs, the latter being saturated with blood. The front of his clothing was also smeared with blood. He wore no cap and had on a pair of carpet slippers. At the police station the prisoner, Thomas Allen, who was said to be of Zulu origins, told to his captors:

> *It was not my intention to cut the gentleman. It was the girl asked me to come in and stop there. I am very sorry that it happened. When the*

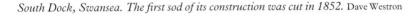

South Dock, Swansea. The first sod of its construction was cut in 1852. Dave Westron

gentleman spoke to me I did not like to tell him that the girl asked me to come there. It is to my regret that it has happened. It was not my bad intention to do anything in a dishonest manner.

An examination of Allen's body revealed that he had a bullet wound in the rear of his right thigh. The shoes that had been found in Mr Kent's bedroom were identified as being his, they having been given to him by a Mrs Murray. The case seemed quite clear cut and, after the usual appearances before the magistrates, Allen was remanded in custody.

At the inquest the facts outlined above were presented as well as some details on the man's background and habits. Mary Jane Shepherd confirmed that Allen was her lodger, when not at sea. However, he was a poor payer of the rent and, after eventually promising to clear his debt, Mrs Shepherd didn't see him again before Detective Inspector Jones turned up making inquiries as to his whereabouts. She was also able to identify a cap and shoes that were found in the Kent's bedroom as belonging to Allen.

Testimony was also heard from John Hill, landlord of the *Queen's Hotel* at Burrows Place. Hill stated that he had become an intimate acquaintance of Allen over the previous few weeks. Allen was a frequent visitor to the *Queen's Hotel* and was last seen there at about 10.15 pm on the fateful Saturday night at which time he left, saying he would be back in five minutes, and leaving three drinks on the bar and not yet paid for. He did not return and Hill only later heard of his arrest.

The next witness was Samuel Paul, a black cook from the *Colombia*. Paul explained that Allen had come on board at around 8.00 am on the Sunday and, from his appearance, it seemed that he had been involved in a fight as there was blood on his cuffs. Paul, who had himself initially appeared to be a possible suspect to the police, also agreed that the slippers that Allen was wearing were ones that he had given him. When Allen had come aboard Paul had already heard about the murder and the fact that the perpetrator had probably been shot. However, when questioned by Paul, Thomas Allen (despite his hidden thigh wound) had been able to run and jump to demonstrate his apparent fitness.

Another witness was Dr William Morgan, MRCS, who stated that he found Mr Kent prostrate on his bed and bleeding profusely from the neck and chest. The throat wound had cut through the trachea with numerous blood vessels being severed. A further wound was found on the right hand side of the chest. It was a deep wound for about five inches of its length, and then became more of a scratch. Another wound had taken a downward direction and had pierced both the chest and lungs. Several smaller wounds were present including at least one to a hand that appeared to have been caused as the victim tried to defend himself. Dr Howell later corroborated the evidence of Dr Morgan and added that he had also extracted a bullet from the right leg of the prisoner. This bullet matched the undischarged rounds remaining in Mr Kent's revolver.

William Morgan, another well known Swansea doctor. West Glamorgan Archive Service

The coroner then summed up the evidence, stating that the jury needed to satisfy themselves on whether Allen was indeed the man who had been in the Kent's room when the crime occurred. If he was, then he must have been there for an unlawful purpose and – even if he were to claim self-defence in the ensuing struggle – the fact that his being there was unlawful would constitute an offence of murder. They also had to consider the possibility, however remote, that the deceased man, for some unknown reason, had inflicted the wounds on himself. If the deceased had not harmed himself then they had to decide whether it was in fact Allen who had inflicted the fatal wounds, or perhaps an as yet unapprehended assailant. The jury was then asked to consider its decision.

Though the jurors made as if to retire, it seems that such was the strength of the evidence against the accused that they had scarcely left the room before they reappeared to accuse the prisoner of the murder of Mr Kent. The prisoner placed his head in his hands and wept.

On 18 March 1889 Allen was brought up for trial at Cardiff before Mr Justice Grantham. When the charge was put to the

prisoner he had replied in a weak voice 'Not guilty'. Mr Arthur
Lewis, for the Crown, stated that Allen had written to Mrs Kent
from prison explaining that he '. . . did not intend to kill your boss
. . .' He went on to say that he was drunk when a girl had suggested
that he go upstairs in the *Gloucester Hotel* and wait for her. She told
him to wait in a certain room and this he did, the girl subsequently
failing to appear, and he hiding under the bed when he heard the
sound of a couple approaching. There, in his drunken state, he had
fallen asleep.

When he awoke he had struck a match being confused as to
where he was. He was then struck by Mr Kent and in the struggle
that followed he admitted using a razor though he did not think at
the time that he '. . . had done so much . . .' with it.

The prosecution posed the question of what was Allen doing in
the room? If his motive had been robbery, and that had resulted in
the death of Mr Kent, then that constituted murder. If his being
there was unlawful and Mr Kent was fatally wounded in an
attempt to detain him, then again that would justify a charge of
murder. As regards intent on the part of the accused, the fact that
Mr Kent was stabbed three times surely indicated a determination to kill. They also noted that Allen was in desperate need of
money if he was to avoid eviction, so that robbery was very much a
possible motive.

The defence team conceded that many of the facts raised by the
prosecution were not disputed. Allen was, indeed, the man who
had fled the room. However, the defence argued that he might
have been there without felonious intent. What if, as Allen had
claimed, he had gone to the room to meet with a girl? Though his
intentions might have been dishonorable towards the lady they
would make him no more than a trespasser. By that yardstick
he did not deserve to be thrown out by force. The defence asked
whether it was plausible that a man intent on robbery would so
easily betray his presence by striking a match in the darkness? It
was accepted that he had inflicted the fatal wounds but this had to
be seen in the context of a violent struggle, instigated by Mr Kent,
that might have been out of all proportion to any unlawful purpose
that had brought Allen into the room.

In summing up the judge pointed to inconsistencies in Allen's
claims. He had at first claimed that it was a servant girl who had
induced him to enter the premises. However, he had later changed
his story so that it was apparently a different female that had

tempted him inside with a promise to follow him shortly. The Judge reiterated that if he was in the room then Mr Kent had a right to kill him, rather than vice versa. Whether the razor was the property of the prisoner or Mr Kent was of no importance though, in fact, it seemed quite certain that it had belonged to Allen.

The jury then retired but took only a few minutes to return a verdict of 'guilty'. The judge, after donning the black cap, then pronounced sentence of death in the usual form. The prisoner was then taken below (where he fainted) before being transferred by horse drawn cab to the Great Western Railway station, and from thence by train to Swansea.

In passing sentence the judge had held out no hope of mercy for the prisoner. That did not, however, prevent the Reverend Oscar Snelling and others from agitating for a reprieve. Any hopes that Allen might have had in that respect were quashed when the Secretary of State declined, after careful consideration, to interfere in the due process of law. If this fact needed underlining in any way, it surely was by the arrival in the town of James Berry, the public executioner, fresh from a hanging in Dublin.

Berry arrived by train at around midnight and proceeded at once to the prison where he inspected the scaffold. This was erected in the exercising room and Berry tested the trap and also met with Allen and took his weight in order that he could estimate the 'drop' required to ensure a speedy despatch. The gallows consisted of a pair of sturdy uprights and a cross beam, standing over a deep pit. A rope dangled from the cross beam. The spot on the boarding where the condemned was to stand was clearly marked. It was a simple, but tried and tested mechanism.

The sun shone on 10 April 1889 as small groups of people gathered outside the prison in Oystermouth Road, Swansea. At 7.00 am Allen was again visited by the Reverend Mr Hudson, to whom he appeared deeply penitent. He seemed resigned to his fate and as cheerful as he could be, given his circumstances. He had left most of a breakfast that consisted of eggs, tea and bread and butter. To help clear his conscience he had written to Mrs Kent and asked for her forgiveness. With commendable magnanimity Mrs Kent had responded to Mr Knight, the prison Governor, as follows:

Will you please let Thomas Allen know, as I hope to be forgiven for my sins, so I forgive him. The rest we must leave to Almighty God, who knows the thoughts of our hearts.

As the time of the execution approached (8.00 am) a crowd of quite some 2,000 persons had gathered outside the prison walls. Berry pinioned Allen's arms and met no resistance as the prison bell tolled in the background. The execution party then entered the room where the gallows stood, while the Reverend Mr Hudson read the service for the dead, the prisoner responding in a subdued manner, walking steadily, and showing no sign of emotion.

With Allen placed on the requisite spot it was left to Berry to ply his deadly trade. He swiftly placed a white cap over Allen's head and the rope around his neck, fixing it just below the left ear. Allen, in a voice now choked with emotion, uttered the words 'Lord Jesus receive my spirit this day' before Berry, with practiced speed, pulled the metal lever that released the trapdoor. Allen immediately plunged into the pit, to a measured drop of six feet and six inches. Apparently possessed of a strong neck, Allen did not die instantly by dislocation of the neck, but rather struggled for almost three minutes before finally falling still. The black flag was raised to the cheers of the assembled crowd outside the prison. As was the usual practice, the body was allowed to hang for an hour before being cut down. The body was then buried within the prison precincts.

The *Cambrian* newspaper carried a full report of the execution, one if its reporters being a witness to the event. Its editorial seemed to be ahead of its time by about seventy years. It stated:

> *Punishment should be deterrent and reformative in character. The death penalty cannot reform the individual who is killed, and the question is often raised whether the fear of hanging is altogether so deterrent of crime as some people honestly believe it to be . . . A certain percentage of executed criminals are convicted on circumstantial evidence, and evidence of this kind is often found to be untrustworthy. Beyond doubt many an innocent man and woman has been so cornered by appearances and statements as to be honestly judged guilty of murder, and so unjustly executed. Such dreadful accidents as these can only be obviated by doing away with the death penalty.*

Whatever the rights and wrongs of the justice system at that time, one thing was certain. There could be no doubt that if anyone was to be executed for the murder of Mr Kent, then that man had to be Thomas Allen.

CHAPTER 13

An Anguished Mind:
The Murder of Mrs O'Neill
1898

Come up, Mrs James, my husband has murdered me.

At about 1.00 am on the 7 July 1898, Police Constable Samuel Thomas was summoned to a house in Powell Street, Swansea. There he found a young girl knocking on the door of the house next door. On seeing the constable she cried:

Officer, come quick, a woman's murdered; come quick upstairs.

Upstairs, Police Constable Thomas found a woman lying on the floor in a pool of blood. The assistance of a doctor was immediately summoned and on questioning the young girl (who was aged about eight years old) it became apparent that the woman was her mother and the wounds had been inflicted by her father. A five-year-old child was also present as was a young baby who lay in the bloodstained bed. The three children were crying bitterly. Their father's whereabouts were at that time unknown.

Doctor Pryce Jones arrived at the scene very quickly and, on examining the woman, found her to have been stabbed eight times, with three of the wounds clearly being of a serious nature. The woman appeared to be semi-conscious and, in her distressed state, was begging to be left to die.

Police Constable Thomas was then assisted by Inspector Parry and Police Constables Pember and Evans. An examination of the crime scene revealed an ordinary knife lying on the kitchen table. The knife was smeared with blood. After some attention from the doctor the woman, identified as being Mrs O'Neill, was removed by an ambulance to the hospital where Doctor Rowlands administered further treatment. It was all to no avail, however, and fifteen minutes after admission Mrs O'Neill passed away.

A search was commenced for Mr O'Neill (also known as 'Price' after his mother's second husband) and, at about 5.00 am, some naked footprints were found on the road leading from the Strand towards the canal. John Croker assisted the search and, with the use of his boat hook, was able to recover the body of Mr O'Neill from the waters of the canal basin. The body was conveyed to the home of Mrs Powell, a neighbour of the O'Neill's in Powell Street, who was prepared to receive it pending further enquiries.

The inquest was speedily convened on the evening of the tragedy before Mr Talfourd Strick, the deputy coroner. The first witness was James Hole who confirmed that he was the father of the deceased who was named Maggie O'Neill. He added that she was thirty two years of age and had been married to Henry O'Neill for about twelve years. They had three children.

A Victorian policeman. Strong and sturdy men were sought for what could be a difficult and dangerous job. South Wales Police Museum

Formerly a seafaring man, O'Neill had worked for the last ten years at the Hafod Works of Vivian and Sons. Some months earlier he had been dismissed due to ill-health. However, on medical advice, he had undertaken a sea trip in the last month which had almost ended in disaster. The ship *Para* had been trapped in the ice off Newfoundland and had subsequently foundered, its sides being stoved in. O'Neill had endured great hardship before being rescued and had returned home to Swansea a week before the awful events at Powell Street. James Hole stated that O'Neill had apparently felt unwell on the Monday before the murder but had regained his composure and health by the Wednesday. Hole regarded O'Neill as a fine son-in-law and thought that only temporary insanity could explain his subsequent actions. He added that O'Neill was of a sober nature and well respected by his workmates.

Sally Ann James was a neighbour who knew that both of the O'Neills had complained of feeling low in spirits during the week of the murder. She had heard some moaning on the morning of the murder and also a child asking 'Oh, mam, mam, what's the matter?' She entered the house of the O'Neill family and called out. Mrs O'Neill replied 'Come up, Mrs James, my husband has murdered me.' Mrs James then ascended the stairs and found the stricken woman on the floor and bleeding heavily. The bed clothes were saturated with blood and Mrs James surmised that the attack must have initially taken place while the deceased was lying in the bed, she having then fallen to the floor in the ensuing struggle.

Elizabeth Phillips, also of Powell Street recalled discussing the Newfoundland shipwreck with the O'Neills, though she noted that Mr O'Neill looked somewhat strange and did not seem to pay any attention to the discussion.

Doctor Pryce Jones testified that the stab wounds had clearly been made with a sharp, pointed instrument. There were serious wounds to the right side of the chest, the right side of the neck and the right shoulder and they were of a form that was consistent with having been made by the bloodstained knife that was found in the house. He had dressed the wounds and also given the victim some brandy, while Mrs O'Neill said 'Let me die' or 'I am dying'. The neck wound was sufficient in its own right to have resulted in death due to loss of blood.

Despite her young age (she was about six years old) Margaret O'Neill, the youngest daughter of the deceased, was called to give evidence. Though she was able to confirm that she had seen a knife similar to that produced at the inquest in the possession of her father she was able to provide no additional evidence. It must be assumed that this was understandably due to her tender years, and the shock of losing both her parents in a single night.

As regards the death of Henry O'Neill, Detective Lewis stated that the footprints found near the canal appeared to have been made by a running man. The body recovered from the water was almost nude and bore no obvious marks of violence. Doctor Pryce Jones was recalled to confirm that the cause of death was drowning.

The deputy coroner then summed up by saying that all available evidence pointed to the man murdering his wife and then committing suicide. The identity of the murderer had been confirmed by Mrs O'Neill's dying statements and as far as could be ascertained the knife belonged to Mr O'Neill. He suggested that the jury would find a verdict of wilful murder and suicide in the respective cases. After a short retirement the jury indeed returned verdicts in accordance with the deputy coroner's recommendations, with the added comment that temporary insanity had played a part.

At this distance in time it is impossible to say what was in the mind of Henry O'Neill when he attacked his wife, seemingly with little or no provocation. As he had returned to sea on medical advice, after a lengthy absence, perhaps there were undeclared issues with his mental well-being.

It seems that he was somewhat depressed at having lost his job with Vivian's. The trip to sea that was supposed to give him a mental lift had had completely the opposite effect when the ship foundered. A crew mate had told the press that O'Neill had managed to save all his kit when the ship went down so there was no question of a loss of valuables affecting his mind. However, the men had been forced to undertake the arduous task of hauling their small boats across the floe ice to safety. Indeed, one man had fallen through what looked like solid ice though he was able to clamber back out, icily cold, with the help of his shipmates. Such dangers were an ever present strain on the mind during the day spent struggling across the fragile ice. The crew were eventually picked up by the *Marina* which also became icebound, albeit temporarily. This ship was also beset with fog during the voyage to safer waters and such additional dangers can have done little to help the already frayed nerves of the rescued men.

O'Neill was reported as having looked 'strange' during the week preceding the murder and possibly the strain of losing his job and then surviving the shipwreck had played on his mind in some unknown way. With no other immediate source of income perhaps the thought of further forced voyages on deep and dangerous waters, in order to simply earn a living wage, was an ever present worry for O'Neill.

Whatever was the underlying cause of his apparent turmoil it had resulted in him murdering his wife in the terrified presence of his children. We can at least be thankful that though his violent and self-destructive actions had orphaned them, at least he had not included them as well in his murderous outburst.

CHAPTER 14

The Case of Sergeant Hopper 1914

I have half a mind to stick the bayonet in you.

A t the approach of Christmas 1914, Swansea, in concert with towns across Britain, was on a war footing. With a great many men already at the front, the role of the Territorial Force had assumed great importance. The Swansea Territorial force (the 6th Welsh) had already departed for France, and its ranks were to be replenished when required by men of a reserve battalion, based at Swansea.

One of the men in the reserve battalion was William Hopper, who had been born in Swansea and was twenty-six years of age. He had seen service with the 3rd and 7th Welsh battalions, including almost three years in South Africa. As such he was already an experienced soldier at the outbreak of war, despite having left the army in 1908 or 1909. He had subsequently found employment in his home town where, obviously having found army life much to his taste, he had joined the Special Reserve of the 3rd Welsh Battalion.

With the outbreak of war in August 1914 Hopper had been speedily recalled to the Colours. His prospect of active service at the front was short lived however, for while stationed at the seaside resort of Porthcawl he suffered a wrist injury that required hospital treatment and led to his discharge on medical grounds. His character was at the time marked as 'good'.

This setback did not dampen Hoppers' martial ambitions, however. In October 1914 he saw an advertisement for a drill instructor with the 6th (Reserve) Battalion based at Swansea and duly submitted his particulars. Experienced men for the army were in short supply and if Hopper could not meet the full rigours of life at the front then his military knowledge would nevertheless be a useful resource for the instruction of raw troops back home. He subsequently secured the post and soon showed his mettle by rising from the rank of corporal to sergeant in a short period. Things were looking up for the young Sergeant Hopper.

As the men of the 6th Reserve Battalion were trained in army discipline and practice at Swansea, opportunities arose for their deployment in roles that allowed a variation in the sometimes monotonous and repetitive training routines. Swansea was an important industrial town with a large number of docks, piers, railway sidings and other industrial facilities. As such it was a potential target for enemy saboteurs, even if the risk of such an attack was in reality quite low. So the trainee soldiers were regularly put through their paces by having to guard and patrol the industrial areas of Swansea. They did this while fully armed with a rifle and bayonet, despite the fact that their rifle training had not yet, in fact, been undertaken. These were troubled times and some short cuts – that would not be countenanced in peacetime – had to be taken to make ends meet.

Thus it was that the newly promoted Sergeant Hopper found himself in charge of a party of armed, and only partly trained, men at the South Dock Pilot House on Christmas Day 1914. His men were to be distributed between four watch posts and a sharp lookout was to be kept all times. Hopper had, of course, acted as a sentry quite often in his earlier days in the army. At that time he had always been instructed to keep his gun loaded while on sentry duty, with a cartridge ready for discharge in the breech. He did not receive any instructions on this point at Swansea and saw no reason to deviate from his former practice. Indeed, he had heard recent reports of shots being fired at sentries in other towns, and having a loaded weapon seemed a sensible precaution in the uncertain times in which he found himself. On what would prove to be a fateful day Hopper was the only man in his squad with any experience of firing a rifle. His men had only recently been equipped with rifles and firing practice was yet to be arranged.

If Hopper was being diligent in applying his former army training to his current position he regrettably overlooked one of its key tenets. While it was customary for a tot of rum to be given to a man prior to going into action at the front, the consumption of alcohol while on other, more peaceful duties, was strictly forbidden. Drinking on duty was rightly frowned upon as alcohol and firearms was a dangerous brew. However, Hoppers duties involved him in boarding ships newly arrived at the dock and checking for the presence of aliens. It was, of course, Christmas Day and the crew of some vessels were keen to display their festive spirit by offering their unexpected visitors a welcoming tot.

On one such vessel Hopper unwisely accepted the offer of some cognac and this was in addition to some beer he had already consumed in the morning. The alcohol certainly had an effect on him and he apparently became a little confused. However, he continued – as best he could – with his duty and, while visiting the No. 8 post at the South Dock he encountered his father, purely by chance. With his father was an acquaintance who gave Hopper a bottle of whisky, a generous gift in wartime Swansea. However, this bottle would prove to be more trouble to Hopper than it was worth.

A little later Hopper realised that his treasured bottle of whisky was missing. One of the men under his command was a private named Enoch Daniel Dudley. A rumour reached the ears of Sergeant Hopper that it was Dudley who had taken his whisky bottle. He then confronted Dudley, demanding to know if the rumour was true to which Dudley replied that he had not stolen it and that his Sergeant was, in fact, a liar. This clearly enraged a slightly befuddled Hopper who told Dudley that he was under arrest, presumably for insubordination, coupled with the suspicion of theft. Adding to Hopper's suspicions was the fact that Dudley appeared to be the worse for drink as did his friend and comrade in arms, Private Gates.

Matters now escalated and the two men closed and fought with each other before Private Gates managed to separate them, though Gates seemed to favour his fellow private in the tussle somewhat more than his sergeant. Dudley then remarked to Hopper 'I have half a mind to stick the bayonet in you.' Hopper wasted little time in summoning assistance by telephoning Sergeant Ryan who in turn alerted Lieutenant Brabazon. Taking control of the tense situation after his arrival, Brabazon ordered that the inebriated Dudley and Gates were to be placed under escort and taken to the nearby Drill Hall. He added that they were to be disarmed and instructed Hopper to ensure that this was done.

The party then set out for the Drill Hall though Lieutenant Brabazon accompanied them only part of the way. During a brief halt at the Wind Street bridge Hopper noticed that Brabazon's injunction that the men were to be disarmed had not been carried

Wind Street, Swansea, looking towards the docks area. Dave Westron

out by members of the escort party. This might have been indicative of the escort party's sympathy for their comrades' predicament. Dudley, in particular, was still wearing his bayonet and side arms. Hopper then reissued his lieutenant's instruction to the escorts but, a little further up Wind Street, he noticed that Dudley still had his side arms on his person.

Frustrated by his orders being apparently ignored Hopper now asked Dudley directly to give up his arms, to which Dudley retorted 'I won't' and added that he was again considering sticking his bayonet into the Sergeant. Challenged again by Hopper, Dudley made as if to take out his bayonet, apparently in a manner that appeared threatening. Hopper exclaimed 'Halt! Left turn!' which resulted only in more mumbled threats from Dudley. Private Reynolds now stepped forward, attempting to defuse the situation by disarming the recalcitrant Dudley. At this Dudley remarked 'What if I refuse?', at which point Hopper raised his rifle, which had a bayonet affixed to it, in what – he would later claim – was a purely defensive gesture, fearing that Dudley might be about to put his threats to use his own bayonet into action. Moments later a shot rang out and struck Dudley. Such was the muzzle velocity of the bullet that, with Dudley only feet away, it pierced his body and then struck Gates. The bullet had come from the rifle of Sergeant Hopper.

The noise of the gunshot brought George Henry Llewellyn, licensee of the *Mansel Arms*, to the scene. Llewellyn was a former police constable and immediately attempted to ascertain what had transpired between the khaki clad group that had resulted in two men being wounded. Hopper frankly admitted having shot them, but added that they had been on the brink of mutiny. At this juncture the stricken and prostrate Dudley turned over slightly and gave a groan before expiring from his wound. The single shot had entered Dudley's body between the second and third ribs on the left side of the chest. It had eventually struck the shoulder blade having on its way pierced the left lung, wind pipe, right bronchus and right lung. Death had been practically instantaneous. A whisky bottle was later found in his trouser pocket. Gates's wound was not so serious, though he too was lying on the ground.

At around this time Police Constable Alfred Skinner arrived and had his attention directed by Llewellyn to Hopper. 'That's right' said Hopper, confirming that he was the dead man's assailant, before adding, 'The deed is done; it can't be undone.' Police Constable Skinner then disarmed Hopper and escorted the sergeant to the police station, with Hopper remarking on the way, 'I am sorry. I had to do it to defend myself. He attacked me first.' Hopper did have a slight wound on his face but this could have been caused in the earlier incident with Dudley. At the police station he added, perhaps unwisely, given the situation in which he found himself 'They were coming over from the docks. They wanted to fight me over there. In Wind Street they started again. One of them struck me in the face, so I shot him. I am sorry for him. One is dead. I did it in self defence.' The subsequent Coroner's inquest had considered the shooting deliberate, but without the intention of actually causing death. However, in March 1915, as a result of the Christmas Day incident, Sergeant Hopper stood trial on a charge of murder at the Glamorgan Assizes, at Cardiff. It would be for a jury to decide whether the offence, if proven, constituted manslaughter or murder.

At the trial the jury members had the events of the night outlined to them. Witness Thomas Nicholls, a motor body builder, had been walking up Wind Street at the time of the alleged murder. He claimed to have seen one of the escorted men with a bayonet in his grasp. A little later he stated that he saw the sergeant bring his rifle to his shoulder and deliberately fire a single shot at a nearby soldier. When questioned on this point Nicholls argued that such an action was in no way accidental. Indeed, he had crossed the road and confronted Hopper with the fact that he had killed the man. Hopper allegedly replied that 'The . . . ought to have been dead before.' Hopper also claimed to have been struck in the face by one of the men, who he described as being 'mutinous'.

Another witness, William George Huxtable, claimed that Hopper, in answer to a question posed by an unknown man, replied 'Oh, mutiny.' Hopper then explained to this mystery man what had happened and Huxtable heard the gentleman tell Hopper 'You did your duty', a comment that Hopper quickly agreed with, also adding, for the benefit of a nearby soldier, that 'It is time the . . . was dead.' Hopper denied making such a statement. In fact he said that he did not remember mentioning mutiny or stating that it was time that Dudley was dead. He told the court that, after the trauma of the night, it was three or four days before he re-gathered his composure and made sense of his actions.

Mr Ellis Griffith, for the prosecution, found it peculiar that whilst the sergeant had quite clear recollections of the period before the fatal shooting, he had no memory at all of what had afterwards transpired. Several witnesses had recounted how Hopper had appeared to have taken deliberate aim at Dudley, killing him and wounding Gates in the process. Immediately after the event Hopper had claimed that he had done his duty in response to a potential mutiny among the men under his command. It was only later, very conveniently said the prosecution, that he had suggested that it had all been a tragic accident. The jury should think carefully on these facts which tended to show that Hopper was indeed guilty of the murder of the unfortunate Dudley.

The case for the defence was put by Mr Llewelyn Williams. He argued that the facts of the case showed that the incident had been nothing more than a tragic accident. Had Hopper wished to bring Dudley to any harm, for whatever reason, then he could have easily chosen a much more sophisticated method than to apparently murder him in full view of numerous witnesses. What was the motive for the alleged crime? If it had been because of the unseemly spat that had occurred between Hopper and Dudley earlier in the day then why did Hopper bring it to the attention of his superiors by telephone? Indeed, at the inquest on the dead man, both Lieutenants Harold Williams and Robert Brabazon had adjudged Hopper to be sober, though admittedly he had been drinking.

It was known that Dudley was the worse for drink and that he had repeatedly refused to surrender his bayonet. Who was to say that he might not run amok at any moment? Another point of emphasis for the defence was that there was no question of pre-meditation. On each occasion that he was questioned by the military authorities (with whom he was familiar) Hopper had referred to the incident as being an accident. It was understandable perhaps, that when constantly pestered by representatives of the civilian authority, his answers were not quite as precise and had led to speculation and misinterpretation.

In his summing up the judge, Mr Justice Atkin, who was con-ducting his first murder trial, stressed that the circumstances of the case did not warrant a reduction of the charge from murder to

Witnesses at Hopper's trial wait outside the court. South West Wales Media. *South Wales Daily Post*

manslaughter. The point on which the case turned was whether the shot was deliberate or accidental. Were it the former then the charge of murder was proved and the guilty party must expect the full retribution of the law. However, were it an accident then the accused must be acquitted. As an aside on the case the judge referred to the evidence that had been presented as to the drinking that had taken place on the day. While this was most regrettable it was not a matter with which the jury should concern itself, advised the judge.

The jury retired to consider its verdict at 4.40 pm and it was not until 6.00 pm that an intimation was received in the court that a verdict had been reached. The jury then re-entered the court and its foreman, evidently in a state of heightened emotion, announced the verdict. It was 'guilty', but with a recommendation to mercy. However, a verdict of guilty in a murder trial in 1915 could result in only one sentence. The judge – after stating that he thought that Hopper's impaired judgement due to drink was at the root of the case – duly donned the black cap and pronounced the solemn words of the death sentence. He added, however, that he would convey the strong feelings of the jury that mercy should be applied in the case to the relevant authorities.

Standing in the dock and watched by several of his khaki-clad comrades, Hopper did not flinch as sentence was imposed. His wife, Ethel, had travelled alone from Swansea to observe the proceedings, which she did without uttering a word or showing any emotion. It was only when she reached the court refreshment room after sentence had been passed that she collapsed under the strain that the proceedings had placed on her frail shoulders.

Within days of sentence being passed sympathy for Hopper was spreading through the town of Swansea. The *South Wales Daily Post*, in its edition of 13 March 1915, featured details of a petition that was being circulated across Swansea. The petition noted that the trial jury had made a recommendation for mercy, but this seemed to have been overlooked when sentence was passed. It pointed out that Hopper was a young married man who had previously been a soldier of good character. It recognised that he had been drinking on the day in question but stressed that there was no hint of premeditation on his part in an incident of very short duration. The petitioners hoped that the authorities would respectfully call on the King to exercise his Royal prerogative and reprieve Sergeant Hopper.

Duplicate

H. M. Prison, Swansea

PARTICULARS of the Conviction of a Soldier, Member of Territorial Force, an Army Pensioner, or a Member of the Army Reserve, now confined in the above-named Prison under a Sentence imposed by a Court other than a Military Court.

Name of Prisoner..............	William Hopper No 2504
Whether Soldier, Member of Territorial Force, Pensioner, or Member of Reserve	Territorial
Regiment in which the Prisoner was serving at the time of his Committal, or in which he had last served. (For Infantry the Battalion should be specified, for Artillery the Battery or Company, and for other Corps the Company.)	6th Batt. The Welsh Regt.
* If a Reservist or Pensioner, Paymaster from whom he last received pay or Pension	✓
Date of Discharge from the Army, or transfer to Reserve	✓
Date of Arrest	25·12·14
Period of Detention awaiting Trial....	56 Days
Date of Conviction...............	2·3·15
Description of Court	assizes
Date of Offence	25·12·14
Place of Offence.............	Swansea
Particulars of Offence, as charged in Commitment	Murder. (Since reduced to Manslaughter) (by Court of Criminal Appeal)
Whether Convicted of a Felony or a Misdemeanour	Felony
Sentence................	Death — reduced to 4 years &c
Court by which Convicted	Glam. assizes
Earliest possible date and hour of Discharge	✓
Date of expiration of Sentence and hour of Discharge	1·3·19
Place of residence before Conviction ...	132 Pentregethin Road, Cwmbwrla. Swansea
Proposed place of residence after Discharge	✓

* This information to be obtained from the Prisoner.

&c Gibbons   Governor.

Date, 29·4·15

For instructions as to transmission, see other side.

P.T.O.

Prison record relating to William Hopper. The National Archives

Happily for Sergeant Hopper the proper authorities did indeed listen when the Court of Criminal Appeal convened an appeal hearing on 29 March 1915 and, after reviewing the case, substituted a finding of manslaughter in place of that of murder. The sentence was then changed from death by hanging to one of four years penal servitude. The case against Hopper in respect of his having wounded Private Gates had not been proceeded with, presumably on the basis that the four year sentence in respect of Dudley was quite sufficient to cover the entire incident.

The army had not quite finished with Sergeant Hopper, however. Army regulations took a very dim view of soldiers who were unable to attend to their duties due to incarceration by the civil authorities and Hopper was duly discharged from the forces on 13 May 1915.

He was due for release from prison on 1 March 1919. We will never truly know whether the incident was a simple accident or a wilful act on the part of Hopper, angry at a man who had fought with him, challenged his authority, and stolen his whisky. Perhaps it was indeed the demon drink that had ultimately caused both men to temporarily act out of character and with such tragic results.

Select Bibliography and Other Sources

Books

Alban, J R, *The Three Nights' Blitz – Select Contemporary Reports Relating to Swansea's Air Raids of February 1941* (City of Swansea, 1994).

Breathnach, Seamus, *The Riddle of the Caswell Mutiny* (Universal Publishers, 2003).

Edwards, Ifan Owen, *A Catalogue of Star Chamber Proceedings Relating to Wales* (University Press Board Cardiff, 1929).

Gabb, Gerald (ed.), *Mr. Dillwyn's Diary* (Swansea Museums Service, 1998).

Gabb, Gerald, *Jubilee Swansea II* (Gerald Gabb, 1999).

Greenlaw, Joanna, *The Swansea Copper Barques and Cape Horners* (Joanna Greenlaw, 1999).

Griffiths, Ralph A (ed.), *The City of Swansea, Challenges and Change* (Alan Sutton, 1990).

Hey, David (ed.), *The Oxford Companion to Local History* (Oxford University Press, 1996).

Holdsworth, W A, *The Handy Book of Parish Law* (1859, reprinted by the Wiltshire Family History Society, 1995).

Hunt, W W, *To Guard My People* (1957).

Jones, W H, *The History of the Lordship of Gower, Volume II* (Royal Institution of South Wales, 1992).

Jones, W H, *History of the Port of Swansea* (facsimile, reprinted by the West Glamorgan County Archive Service, 1995).

Molloy, Pat, *And they Blessed Rebecca* (Gomer Press, 1983).

Morris, Bernard, *Swansea Castle* (City and County of Swansea, 2000).

Rogers, W C, *A Pictorial History of Swansea* (Gomer Press/W C Rogers, 1981).

Spolasco, Baron, *The Narrative of The Wreck of the Killarney* (Baron Spolasco, 1839, digitised by books.google.com).

Thomas, Sandra, *George Grant Francis of Swansea 1814–1882* (West Glamorgan County Archive Service, 1993).

Thomas, W S K, *The History of Swansea – from Rover Settlement to the Restoration* (Gomer Press, 1990).

Whitman, Walt, Holloway, Emory and Adimari, Ralph, *New York Dissected* (R R Wilson, 1932).

Wiliams, David, *The Rebecca Riots – a Study in Agrarian Discontent* (Cardiff University of Wales Press, 1955).

Williams, Glanmor (ed.), *Swansea – an Illustrated History* (Christopher Davies, 1992).

Articles

The Welsh History Review, Vol. 22, No. 4, *Wales and the 'Bloody Code': the Brecon Circuit of the Court of Great Sessions in the 1750s*, John Minkes.

Medical History, 1986, No. 30, *Yellow Fever in South Wales*, 1865, C E Gordon
   Smith & Mary E Gibson.

Periodicals and Newspapers
The Brooklyn Daily Eagle
The Bristol Mercury
The Cambrian
The Cheltenham Examiner
The Cork Examiner
The Daily News (London)
The Gentleman's Magazine
The Gloucester Journal
The Medical Circular
The New York Daily Tribune
The New York Evening Post
Report of the Medical Officer of the Privy Council (1866, House of Commons Printed
   Papers)
South Wales Daily Post
The Times
The Western Mail

Websites
www.flickr.com/photos/brizzlebornandbred/sets/ (Paul Townsend)
www.gtj.org.uk
www.penllergare.org
www.Public.Image.org
www.Rootschat.com
www.Questia.com

Note: Efforts have been made to trace copyright holders but where this has not
proved possible further information on the ownership of specific material will be
welcomed by the author so that future editions can be amended. I can be con-
tacted via the publishers on receipt of a stamped, self-addressed envelope.

Index

Note: The word 'Swansea' appears in numerous pages and has not been indexed except where it refers to something more specific, e.g. Swansea **Castle** etc.